The Authentic Tawney

The Authentic Tawney

A New Interpretation of the Political Thought of R.H.Tawney

Gary Armstrong
& Tim Gray

imprint-academic.com

Published in the UK by Imprint Academic
PO Box 200, Exeter EX5 5YX, UK

Published in the USA by Imprint Academic
Philosophy Documentation Center
PO Box 7147, Charlottesville, VA 22906-7147, USA

ISBN 9 781845 40224 2 Paperback

A CIP catalogue record for this book is available from the
British Library and US Library of Congress

Contents

8. Writings from 1938–1952

9. Conclusion

Chapter One

Introduction

1.1 Executive summary

Conventional interpretations of Tawney's political thought assert that it is characterized by an overwhelming consistency and is a derivative of his Christianity. This has led to the adoption of an approach in which texts separated by decades are raided to generate an essential or integral Tawney, whose political values are stable entities with a theoretical core in the religious-inclined Diaries he kept during 1912–14. This book employs a chronological analysis to demonstrate how such an approach commits the error of what Quentin Skinner has termed the 'mythology of coherence', thereby distorting the nature of Tawney's thought in three ways. First, the commentators assume that there should be coherence between the different formulations of political ideas that Tawney presents. Second, they claim that the organizing source that binds Tawney's political theory together is Christianity. Third, they detect in Tawney's early Diaries the evidence for such a binding source. However, the truth is that Tawney is not bound to produce a coherent political theory; that while his personal commitment to Christian beliefs remained intact, he abandoned his early doctrine that politics without Christianity was deficient; and that the unpublished Diaries are not a reliable guide to his published thought.

1.2 Tawney's importance

R.H. Tawney's vigorous attack on materialism, *The Acquisitive Society*, and his condemnation of a class-based social system contained in *Equality*, have ensured his place in Labour Party history. Indeed, his prescriptions have influenced a generation of left-wing politicians, inspired by his vision of a harmonious society founded on fellowship, with the means of a civilized existence available to all. Contrary to Cole's prediction (quoted in Wright, 1987: vii) that Tawney's 'destiny is gradually to sink into comparative oblivion, along with some others in history whose personality bulked so much larger than their published work will indicate', his influence was not confined to his lifespan. For instance, two surveys of MPs' reading habits, one conducted by the *New Statesman* in 1996, and the other by *The Guardian* in 2005, rated Tawney as one of the most widely consulted authors amongst Labour politicians. Also, Tawney's name cropped up during the disputes in the UK that surrounded the defection of the 'gang of four' from the Labour Party to found the Social Democratic Party in the 1980s. According to Crewe and King (1995: 34), one of the defectors, William Rodgers, viewed himself as 'standing in the line of ideological descent running from R.H. Tawney through Evan Durbin and Hugh Gaitskell to Anthony Crosland', and the new party established a Tawney society to underline their supposed ancestry. Also, in the supposedly ideologically-free zone that is New Labour, Tawney's work is still invoked in tones of approval, even if his faith in a socialist society seems out of kilter with the Party's current ethos and actions. Indeed, the esteem felt for Tawney in left-wing circles has led commentators to adopt a reverential vocabulary: Annan (1990: 129) claimed that to his followers Tawney was regarded as a 'sage', while in an essay to commemorate the centenary of his birth, Ryan (1980: 408) referred to Tawney as a 'socialist saint'. In their biography of Harold Laski, Kramnick and Sheerman (1993: 251) comment that Tawney's influence on succeeding generations is more profound than that of either Laski or that other great socialist intellectual, G.D.H Cole, despite the fact that after 1931 Tawney wrote very little. Other important contemporary politicians who, when attempting to set out their personal vision, have made use of Tawney include Roy Hattersley (1987), Neil Kinnock (1986), and Shirley Williams (1981).

The sense of Tawney's significance to the British Labour Movement has even been recognized by ideological opponents like Keith Joseph, who described Tawney as being engulfed in an 'ocean of instinctive approval' (Joseph and Sumption, 1979: 2), and by Peregrine Worsthorne, who advised Mrs Thatcher to consult Tawney's works to understand the mindset of her enemies (Wright, 1987: 130). Even W.H. Greenleaf (1983: 439–440), who considers Tawney to be an over-rated and generally inferior thinker, felt compelled to discuss Tawney's thought in his magisterial *The British Political Tradition* because of the esteem in which he is held amongst British socialists.

Given this intimate connection with the Labour movement, and the eulogies that he inspires, Tawney continues to be an important figure in the history of political thought. However, it has been 20 years since the last full-length study of his work was published, and there is a need to engage with Tawney's work from a new perspective, because the most prominent commentators have erroneously presented Tawney as a proponent of a coherent political theory containing political concepts that were based on Christian principles, and were relatively unchanged during nearly 40 years of writing.

1.3 A new approach to Tawney

A new approach to Tawney's political thought is needed to correct three erroneous views that are commonly put forward by his commentators. The first view is that Tawney's work is governed by an overwhelming consistency. This view neglects the extent to which Tawney altered his political conceptualizations. Although there is a thematic persistence in Tawney's work, in that the subject areas that intrigued him as a young man still engaged him in his later years, his conceptions of religion, politics, equality, liberty, rights, and duties were modified in a way that changed the character of his thought. The procedure of regarding Tawney's concepts as systematic structures, with works separated by decades being raided for their contribution to some integral conception of political value, leads to distortion. Treating Tawney chronologically or developmentally, with the integrity of individual texts restored, corrects this erroneous argument and gives a more accurate picture of a thinker whose thought is characterized by change rather than stasis, and development rather than consistency.

The chronological approach also corrects the second erroneous view held by many commentators—that Tawney's politics is a derivative of his Christian faith. While it is true that Tawney was a Christian believer throughout his adult life, and that this had an important impact on his political thought, the character and the extent of that impact changed profoundly. The chronological approach reveals that Tawney significantly diluted the Christian basis of the thinking revealed in the Diaries he kept from 1912 to 1914. In the Diaries, not intended for publication, but posthumously published in 1972 under the title of the *Commonplace Book*, Tawney asserts that key political concepts depend completely upon a belief in a Christian God, and he disparages political activity from a stance of religious high-mindedness. However, it will be demonstrated that the doctrines set out in the Diaries, far from confirming the religious basis of Tawney's thought or, more extremely, serving as the hidden core of Tawney's subsequent writings, were gradually abandoned as Tawney adopted more secular stances in his published work, tempering the extent of Christian ideas in his political thought. Thus, the chronological approach also corrects the third erroneous assertion in the conventional interpretation of Tawney — that the Diaries provide the key to understanding the religious foundations of Tawney's subsequent political theory.

The chronological approach offers a more authentic interpretation than the essentialist approach, by presenting Tawney's political theory in all its tergiversations. It will be shown that there is a residual fuzziness in Tawney's enunciation of concepts such as religion, politics, equality, liberty, rights, duties and democracy, and that the pursuit of an essentialist Tawney produces an artificial and contrived cohesion. Tawney's lack of consistency and constancy on these subjects is a fundamental aspect of his thought, which requires acknowledgment, not supercession. The next section highlights the work of the most prominent commentators who put forward these three erroneous viewpoints in the conventional or 'essentialist' or 'integral' interpretation of Tawney's political thought—the sort of viewpoints which Quentin Skinner (1969: 16) has argued illustrate 'the mythology of coherence'.

1.4 Commentators who make the three erroneous assumptions of the essentialist approach to Tawney's political thought

Three major commentators are highlighted here for making these three erroneous assumptions of the essentialist approach to Tawney's political thought—Anthony Wright, who makes all three assumptions; and W.H. Greenleaf and Ross Terrill, who make the first and second assumptions, and (partly) the third. In addition, J.M. Winter (1974), who played a significant editorial role in Tawney scholarship, makes all three assumptions, as do both G. Dale (2000) and M. Carter (2003). G. Foote (1985) makes the first and second assumption, while D. Reisman (1987) makes the second assumption.

1.4.1 Anthony Wright's essentialist interpretation of Tawney

Anthony Wright (1987: 26) claims that Tawney's work displays a 'massive unity, consistency and coherence' (the first erroneous assertion). Wright (1987: 70; 2; 19) describes Tawney's doctrine of the equal valuation of all humanity as creatures of God as 'the inner core of his whole structure of personal and social morality'; locates that core in Christianity, affirming its 'overwhelming centrality'; and states categorically that 'There is no reason today why, in seeking to understand the basis of Tawney's thought, there should be any uncertainty on this point… it forms the unstated inner core of

Tawney's published work. It is not just that he believed in the existence of God (as a fact of experience), nor in Christianity as the per-
sonification of God, revealing his nature, but that he held these
beliefs to be the indispensable basis for a true morality'. This is the
second erroneous assumption—claiming that Christianity is the
unchanging single organizing idea that runs throughout Tawney's
political theory.

Wright (1987: 19; 136; 30) acknowledges that Tawney's published
writings are 'generally not framed in Christian terms or presented
as exemplifications of Christian doctrines' — indeed, Tawney con-
structs 'a public case for socialism in which God was conspicuous
by his absence' — but Wright argues that this is only because of tactical reasons. The *Commonplace Book* is the work of a man operating
outside the public arena, content in his privacy to display his conscience and the fundamental basis of his beliefs. By contrast, the
published works are those of an eminently practical man concerned
to assist the foundation of a new social order, recognizing in an
increasingly secular society that the act of persuasion cannot be
accomplished by mere faith. The task for Tawney, the prescriptive
social theorist, is to 'persuade people who do not naturally share his
own fundamental grounds, those of Christian morality, for rejecting the existing social order' (Wright, 1987: 30). According to
Wright, then, whilst Tawney's critique of capitalism is derived
from religious doctrine, the statement of this is not sufficiently compelling to generate the will for socialist change, so Tawney reverts
to a secular idiom.

Finally, Wright makes the third erroneous assumption by attributing a crucial role to the *Commonplace Book* (or Diaries) in justifying
the second assumption. According to Wright (1987: 19), the works
that Tawney selected for publication are generally inconclusive and
ambiguous in revealing the presuppositions that governed his politics, an opacity that is only dispelled by the Diaries. In Wright's thesis, the *Commonplace Book* becomes the central resource in deciding
that Tawney's politics is largely a derivative of his religious principles. The posthumous publication of the Diaries unlocked the
secret which made Tawney's political theory coherent—his profound commitment to Christian values, which he was only able to
express in his private jottings. According to Wright, by demonstrat-

ing Tawney's profound commitment to Christian ethics, the *Commonplace Book* performs the crystallizing role of making explicit the religious assumptions that governed the concepts used in the political works. Responding to Beatrice Webb's incomprehension at Tawney's commitment to Christianity, Wright (1987: 19) states that 'If Beatrice and others had seen Tawney's own diary the mystery would have been solved'. So Wright casts the Diaries in the role of providing the theoretical foundations of Tawney's political doctrine. Essentially, the reflections before the First World War form the lens through which to understand, and interpret, Tawney's subsequent intellectual output. It is assumed by Wright that the private nature of the Diaries frees Tawney from the constraints imposed by an audience, enabling him to express himself with absolute candour. On this interpretation, the Diaries have an authenticity that is lacking in the published works, and this justifies Wright's elevation of them to the status of the central key to a full understanding of the Tawney project.

1.4.2 W.H. Greenleaf's essentialist interpretation of Tawney

Greenleaf (1983: 448) makes the first erroneous assumption—that Tawney's political theory is coherent—in claiming that, in 1952, Tawney 'was still of opinion that the basic impulse behind British Socialism' was '"unashamedly ethical"... This... was broadly the Christian- and morality-based approach to political and social change that Tawney was working out in the years immediately before the Great War'. The second erroneous assumption is made by Greenleaf (1983: 452) implicitly in the above quotation, and explicitly in asserting that Tawney's Christian moralism exerts a 'continuous formative influence' on his work. Indeed, according to Greenleaf (1983: 443), Tawney's political thought is largely a derivative of his religious beliefs: 'His ideas were founded on a sincere and fervent acceptance of the essential truth of Christian doctrine'. In Tawney's theory, says Greenleaf (1983: 444), 'Always... genuine social progress and the proper and ultimate context of political judgement alike rest on the spiritual insight of Christian morality'. For example, Greenleaf (1983: 452) says that 'the heart of his [Tawney's] attack on Capitalism hinges on an accusation of its incompatibility with Christian principle'. Moreover, Greenleaf (1983: 451) claims that, in his writings between 1921 and 1929, Tawney calls for 'the elaboration of "nothing less than Christian sociology"'.

Greenleaf (1983: 443) partly makes the third erroneous assumption in that, although, unlike Wright, he does not assign a primary role to the Diaries in creating this Christian coping, he does say that the Diaries underpin the Christian belief system that can be gleaned from the published writings: 'The new data made available by the recent publication of this pre-war journal considerably reinforce this understanding and... make clearer the particular nature of Tawney's beliefs in this regard'. It is true that Greenleaf (1983: 449) acknowledges (a) that Tawney's experiences during the First World War stimulated changes in his political thought towards an explicit embrace of the Labour Party and an acceptance of practical reforms; (b) that there is a difference in both content and style between the Diaries (where Tawney is concerned with personal sin) and the published work (where Tawney is concerned with social and political structures); and (c) that the 'continuous formative influence of Christian moralism' on Tawney's political thought does not depend on the musings contained in the Diaries (the works that Tawney selected for publication are seen by Greenleaf to be fully expressive of a Christian disposition; the *Commonplace Book* merely corroborates what is already evident). Nevertheless, Greenleaf (1983: 449) is adamant that the fundamental themes of the Diaries represent the conceptual foundations that shape the later Tawney writings: 'the later studies presuppose and may be seen to exemplify in particular and important respects, conceptions of morality and divine justice in which he had come to believe and which are, often so starkly, reflected in the pages of the diary'.

1.4.3 Ross Terrill's essentialist interpretation of Tawney

Ross Terrill (1973: 8) makes the first erroneous assumption in stating that a 'way of demystifying Tawney is to try and make a systematic construction out of Tawney's assorted writings about socialism'. Terrill (1973: 8–9) says that this amounts to privileging the analytical approach over the chronological approach: 'If Tawney's socialism is still to stand, its intellectual and moral foundations must be made explicit. This consideration has prompted a basically analytical treatment, which assumes a certain constant core in Tawney, rather than a basically chronological treatment, which maps in detail the changes in his position over the years'. Terrill (1973: 9–10) defends his essentialist approach on the grounds that 'Because Tawney's manner has an intellectual meaning, it does not seem an undue distortion of Tawney's total significance to make a systematic construction of his thought'. In Terrill's book, concepts are treated as static composite entities, made up by liberally quarrying quotations from throughout Tawney's work, with no distinction drawn between the young and the mature writer, or between the unpublished and the published writings. Terrill (1973: 250; 260) claims that there is consistency in Tawney's arguments: 'Tawney, although he varied his exposition for each challenge, met all with essentially the same arguments… Tawney's general line of analysis came from the foundations of his long-established socialist position'.

Yet Terrill devotes nearly half his book to Tawney's biography, where he describes at length Tawney's gradual shift away from religion in his writings. In fact, Terrill (1973: 9) seeks to justify his static analysis of Tawney's political theory by saying that his biographical chapters cover the changes in Tawney's thinking: 'To lessen the pitfalls of this approach, the biographical chapters (Part One) attend to the development of Tawney's thought through the various stages of his life'. But this justification only compounds the problem for Terrill, because it draws attention to changes in Tawney's thinking that he fails to consider in his conceptual analysis. The biographical chapters in Terrill's book do not provide chronological compensation for his static conceptual analysis, because the development of Tawney's political thought can only be understood by explaining the consequential changes in his argumentation. While the account of Tawney's life can give the reader clues to the circumstances that helped to induce the changes, this is not sufficient unless the conceptual changes are themselves elaborated. So the biographical narrative and the conceptual assessment are not mutually reinforcing but mutually conflicting: they are working to different purposes which undermine the integrative approach espoused by Terrill. He is in the strange position of indicating a change, but unable to deal with it because of the assumption of conceptual constancy in his analytical section. He is imprisoned by his adherence to a deficient methodology.

This dilemma is graphically illustrated by Terrill's account of Tawney's treatment of religion. In his biographical narrative, Terrill (1973: 60) demonstrates how Tawney's attitude towards Christianity and the Church varied over time, until, eventually, 'his theology slipped to the unexamined corners of his mind'. However, this unfolding and varied interaction of the secular and the religious in Tawney's life is not carried over into Terrill's conceptual analysis of Tawney's political thought in the second part of the book. Terrill neglects to represent the dynamic interplay between the religious and the worldly in the core concepts that Tawney developed over a long intellectual career. Moreover, despite his care not to exaggerate the role of Christianity in Tawney's political thought, and his assiduity in showing throughout the analytical chapters on concepts such as property, social function and citizenship how they are the product of a number of influences, Terrill still maintains that without the widespread acceptance of Christian assumptions, such concepts would be of little significance. So with the biographical and conceptual sections exhibiting radically different views on the relationship between Tawney's politics and religion, Terrill's essentialist approach, far from producing a coherent understanding of Tawney's work, itself falls into incoherence.

The second erroneous assumption is made by Terrill (1973: 8) in portraying Christianity as the organizing principle of this systematic construction: 'It becomes important today, if it was not for Tawney, to understand how much of his socialism was derived from his Christianity'. According to Terrill (1973: 246–247), 'If it is not certain that he derived his socialism wholly from Christianity, he *located* it within Christianity'. Terrill (1973: 249) holds that 'Christian belief gave a vital margin of meaning to a number of Tawney's ideas', and without acceptance of Christian assumptions some of Tawney's political concepts would be undermined. For example, the equal worth of all human beings would be left unsupported, and thereby the necessity for redistribution of wealth from rich to poor would no longer be compelling. According to Terrill (1973: 248–249), 'Aspects of Tawney's socialist appeal have consequently lost their power with the decline of Christianity... If men are not intrinsically of equal worth, as Christianity teaches, why should rewards not go to the brightest and the best citizens, without regard for the resulting gap in living standards between them?'

Terrill partly makes the third erroneous assumption by lumping the Diaries in with the rest of Tawney's works as a source of raw material for his conceptual analysis of Tawney's political theory. So although the Diaries are not given a special status in unlocking the secret of the integral Tawney, neither are they excluded from the analysis as unreliable sources of the views of the mature Tawney. Indeed, Terrill (1973: 46) praises the acuity of the *Commonplace Book*: 'In Manchester he kept a diary — alas, for less than two years — concerned above all with the march of his thoughts on moral principles and the social order. It is earnest and acute, vigorous in aspiration, sharp in argument, with little of the brittle filigree that gives a ponderous touch to the late Tawney'.

1.4.4 Other commentators

Other contributors to Tawney scholarship make one or more of the three erroneous assumptions. For example, Winter makes all three assumptions. He claims, first, that Tawney's theory was consistent: 'The stability of Tawney's outlook is its most striking characteristic. His post-war writings bear the same distinctive marks of the moral approach to socialism which he had outlined a decade earlier in his Commonplace Book' (Winter, 1974: 284). Winter (1972: xxii) asserts that Tawney's theory was set in stone before the First World War: 'He had already made his mind up on the moral questions which dominated his life's work... his fundamental position... remained unshaken'. Second, Winter (1972: xiv) argues that Christianity lay permanently at the heart of Tawney's project, referring to 'Tawney's attempt to articulate that voice of reason or, in his terms, that voice of Christian morality, and to follow its guidance in the construction of an outline of his life's work as a historian and social critic'. Third, Winter (1972: xiii) sees the Diaries as the key to Tawney's theory: 'R.H.Tawney was a man of deep Christian beliefs and powerful emotions, and nowhere can we gain as full a view of his mind and temperament... as in the Commonplace Book or diary which he kept at Manchester from 1912 to 1914... [It is] a unique record of the assumptions which supported Tawney's lifelong work as a socialist and as a scholar'.

Similarly, Dale (2000: 92; 88–89), in his assessment of the Christian contribution to the Labour Party, reiterates all three erroneous assumptions, asserting that Tawney, as early as 1914, had 'developed a unified framework for his work', and had espoused 'a Christian-inspired revolution for equality and liberty'. Whilst Dale (2000: 95) acknowledges that Tawney's faith 'remained personal', he is emphatic that 'Christianity remained the core of his philosophy', with the Commonplace Book providing the 'clearest expression of his religious and political faith'.

Likewise, if less explicitly, Carter (2003: 171–184) makes all three assumptions. First, he effectively embraces the consistency thesis by adopting a mode of analysis that treats Tawney's concepts of rights, equality, freedom and the role of the state as static, integral entities. For instance, Carter (2003: 175) asserts that Tawney 're-jected the notion of natural rights' and stated that 'all rights were conditional and derivative', and needed to be 'put to the test of social justification'. Thus Carter extracts an argument advanced in *The Acquisitive Society*, and magnifies it to serve as a general classification of Tawney's theory of rights, without acknowledging Tawney's later distinction between primary and secondary rights. Second, Carter (2003: 176; 172; 173) asserts the primacy of Christianity in Tawney's works: although he is more concerned to assert the impact of Idealism on Tawney's thought, it is the religious aspects of the philosophy that Carter highlights, stressing that Tawney's 'moral beliefs were rooted in a view of Christianity that was, as with many of the idealists, essentially immanentist', and claiming that it was this religious impulse that 'placed equality firmly at the centre of his political philosophy', as demonstrated by his discussion of equal worth in the *Commonplace Book*. The third erroneous assumption (according a vital role to the Diaries) is implicitly made by Carter in this last assertion.

Foote makes the first and second erroneous assumptions. In asserting Tawney's consistency, Foote draws a distinction between Tawney's various political stances and his overarching philosophy. Foote (1985: 72) acknowledges that Tawney's political position 'shifted radically over time', with his early endorsement of guild socialism in the twenties, his acceptance, and subsequent rejection, of gradualism in the late twenties and early thirties, and his embrace of revisionism in the fifties. However, according to Foote, these distinctive platforms were in a 'fundamental sense superficial', serving as tactical manoeuvres to promote a 'coherent socialist philosophy which transcends any particular political situation', and in this deeper sense, Tawney's 'mature political thought never *really* changed' (Foote, 1985: 72). Whilst the reference to 'mature' implies a distinction within Tawney's work, Foote (1985: 76) does not elaborate it, and instead firmly anchors Tawney's fundamental position in a social Christianity that is the 'core of his social philosophy in whatever political guise it presented itself'.

Reisman (1987: 26) makes the second erroneous assumption, in urging that one thing 'to remember about Tawney is the Christian nature (more often implicit than explicit)… of his social theory'. According to Reisman (1987: 31), 'Tawney's own ultimate value is the desirability of applying the Christian perspective not just in matters of personal morality but to questions of society and its structure as well'.

1.5 Theoretical reasons for rejecting the three erroneous assumptions

These three erroneous assumptions should be corrected because they distort Tawney's political theory. Such distortions are inevitable because each of the assumptions breach basic principles of legitimate interpretation in the history of political thought. In other words, there are theoretical reasons for rejecting them.

1.5.1 *The assumption of coherence in Tawney's political theory is tendentious*

Quentin Skinner (1969: 16) exposes the fallacy of assuming that a political theorist's work *must* be coherent; this is the 'mythology of coherence':

> It may be (and indeed it very often happens) that a given classic writer is not altogether consistent, or... fails... to give any systematic account of his beliefs... it will become dangerously easy for the historian to conceive it as his task to supply or find in... these texts the coherence which they may appear to lack... the consequent temptation [is] to find a 'message' which can be abstracted from it and more readily communicated... The inevitable result... will be a form of writing which might be labelled the mythology of coherence. The writing of the history of ethical and political philosophy is pervaded by this mythology.

Skinner (1969: 16-17) provides illustrations of the myth of coherence in commentaries on Hooker, Hobbes, and Hume:

> Thus if 'current scholarly opinion' can see no coherence in Hooker's *Laws*, the moral is to look harder, for 'coherence' is surely 'present'. If there is doubt about the 'most central themes' of Hobbes' political philosophy, it becomes the duty of the exegete to discover the 'inner coherence of his doctrine' by reading the *Leviathan* a number of times until... he finds that its argument has 'assumed some coherence'. If there is no coherent system 'readily accessible' to the student of Hume's political works, the exegete's duty is 'to rummage through one work after another' until the 'high degree of consistency in the whole corpus' is duly displayed... 'at all costs'... the ambition is always to 'arrive' at a 'unified interpretation', to 'gain' a 'coherent view of an author's system'.

Such treatment, says Skinner (1969: 17-18), may project upon a political theory an artificial coherence which may bear little relation to the intention of its author:

> This procedure gives the thoughts of various classic writers a coherence, and an air generally of a closed system, which they may never have attained or even meant to attain... The history thus written becomes a history not of ideas at all, but of abstractions: a history of thoughts which no one actually succeeded in thinking, at a level of coherence which no one ever actually

attained... the astonishing, but not unusual, assumption [is made] that it may be quite proper, in the interests of extracting a message of higher coherence from an author's work, to discount the statements of intention which the author may have made about what he was doing.

Skinner (1969: 19–20) shows how seemingly self-contradictory elements in a theorist's work are interpreted as not truly contradictions at all: 'any apparent contradictions which the given writer's work does seem to contain... cannot really be contradictions... The explanation... that an apparent contradiction may simply be a contradiction... seems not to be considered. Such apparent contradictions... should not simply be left in their unresolved state, but should be made to serve instead in helping toward "a fuller understanding of the whole theory" — of which the contradictions... form only an unsublimated part'. According to Skinner (1969: 20), the possibility that contradictions might indicate a change in the theorist's thinking is not even considered by these commentators: 'The very suggestion... that the "contradictions and divergences" of a given writer may be "supposed to prove that his thought had changed" has been dismissed by a very influential authority as just another delusion'. For example, in studying Machiavelli's political thought, instead of 'anything so straightforward as an attempt to indicate the nature of the developments and divergences from the *Prince* to the late *Discourses*', it has been 'insisted that the appropriate task must be to construct for Machiavelli a scheme of beliefs sufficiently generated for the doctrines of the *Prince* to be capable of being... [integrated] into the *Discourses* with all the apparent contradictions resolved' (Skinner 1969: 20).

We argue that several commentators, by searching for the 'inner coherence' of Tawney's political thought, have unwittingly embraced Skinner's 'mythology of coherence', thereby producing artificial, abstract, and distorted interpretations of his work.

1.5.2 The assumption that Christianity is the cohering agent in Tawney's political theory ignores weighty evidence of change in the basis of his ideas

While Tawney never lost his personal faith in Christianity, his view of its role in society underwent considerable change from the opinions he expressed in the Diaries to the opinions he expressed in his published works. In his unpublished Diaries, Tawney portrayed Christianity as the source of all morality, including political morality. This doctrine of Christian exclusivity meant that concepts such as equal worth, liberty, rights and duties not only gained strength from Christianity, but were derived from it. Indeed, the notion of human equality was incomprehensible unless deduced from the common fatherhood of God, while liberty was only intelligible in terms of religious austerity and benign subordination to spiritually sanctioned duties (Tawney, 1972: 57). So politics must adhere to Christian virtues if it was ever to emerge from the gutter. However, by contrast, in his published works Tawney gradually disengaged Christianity from its exclusive command of morality, and derived concepts like equality and liberty from secular arguments. For example, in *Equality* (1931), Tawney broadens the justification of equality from the narrow and exclusively Christian basis of the Diaries to a generalized humanist category which is fleshed out in terms of the basic needs of human beings, giving special status to those institutions that serve those needs. The basis for political morality thus draws more on rational argumentation, than faith. The Labour Party was endorsed as a positive instrument for achieving ethically important goals independently of the Christian religion.

Accordingly, it is not convincing to argue, as Wright, Terrill and Greenleaf do, that Tawney's Christian faith is the organizing principle of his political thought. Christianity may have been the organizing principle of the Diaries, but not of Tawney's political thought as a whole. While he himself found socialism fully compatible with Christianity, in his published works he did not try to justify socialism on grounds of Christian values. Neglecting the developmental nature of Tawney's work can only lead to a superficial understanding in which layers of its meaning are lost. The rich diversity of

Tawney's thought and the varying idioms in which he couched his political thought at different times to different audiences, is an integral part of Tawney's project, and can only be reflected by tracing the conception, development and maturation of his political theory. Using the chronological approach, Tawney's concepts are traced from their initial position of overwhelming dependency on religion, to their release from that dependence into a rational, secular application. It is only by charting the progress of his intellectual position in an increasingly secular world that the process of this transition can be understood. The crude methodological foundation of the essentialist approach cannot allow such a dynamic interpretation, because it forces Tawney's political theory into the rigid straitjacket of Christianity.

Wright's explanation that Tawney's secular presentation of his later political ideas was simply a tactical move designed to persuade non-Christian people to accept socialist doctrines, throws doubt on Tawney's intellectual integrity. By privileging the religious derivation of Tawney's politics, but arguing that his concepts were given a secular garb purely for the purpose of persuasion, Wright is devaluing the theoretical content of Tawney's later ideas. According to Wright (1987: 107), Tawney is 'engaged in a politics of moral exhortation rather than social explanation', in that he is more concerned to persuade than explore. But this ignores the more plausible explanation that by detaching Christianity from his analysis of political concepts, Tawney believed that he was strengthening, not weakening, their intellectual credentials by demonstrating that they could be founded on rational argumentation alone. In other words, Tawney deliberately moved from an underdeveloped Christian exclusivity to a developed secular alignment for its explanatory, not its rhetorical, force.

1.5.3 The assumption that the Commonplace Book provides the key to coherence in Tawney's political theory overrides Tawney's own intentions in not publishing the Diaries

Giving the Diaries the status of providing the key to the central organizing idea of Tawney's political theory overrules Tawney's own view of them — as purely private musings compiled during an early period of his life before his understanding of politics had matured. The Diaries contain Tawney's reflections on events happening in the two years before the First World War—reflections that are immediate and emotional rather than considered and rational.

The implications of elevating the status of writings that were never *intended* by Tawney for publication is not dealt with by the commentators. Given Tawney's concern to publish only what was deemed worthy of public presentation, why should the *Commonplace Book* hold any credence as making explicit the basis of Tawney's practical politics? Even Wright (1987: ix) acknowledges that 'Tawney's work, even quite minor pieces, usually went through several versions before seeing light of day... Tawney knew what he wanted to say, and how he wanted to say it'. While we cannot know what Tawney's attitude would have been to the posthumous publication of his diaries, his reaction to a suggestion that he publish a new collection of essays to mark his eightieth birthday is significant. When this request was made, Tawney expressed doubts about whether he had material of sufficient quality to justify another book (Hinden, 1964: 7; Terrill, 1973: 111). Although, despite his reservations, Tawney began tentatively to collect his papers together with a view to publication, his initial reticence re-emerged and the process was never completed, although a posthumous collection of essays was published under the title *The Radical Tradition*, which incorporated a number of the pieces that Tawney had selected. This is instructive on two counts. First, we can reasonably surmise that Tawney was reluctant to sanction the publication of any material he deemed to be inferior. Second, of the pieces that he initially selected, with the exception of an essay on Robert Owen, all had been previously published in one form or another, implying that the remainder of his material, which included the *Commonplace Book*, was not considered worthy of publication.

Winter (1972: xiv) argues that the private nature of the Diaries gives them an air of authenticity because it reveals the *real* Tawney, untainted by the constraints of having to appeal to an audience increasingly less receptive to religious dogma. But it is more convincing to argue that it reveals the views of a writer who has not yet experienced the life events that would change his political thinking.

Moreover, the fact that the *Commonplace Book* tends towards self-clarification, rather than a sustained intellectual argument, raises questions about their admittance to the Tawney canon. The private nature of the diaries actually makes them *less*, rather than *more*, reliable, because in writing them, Tawney was operating independently of an audience, whether academic or political, and therefore without the external discipline to rigorously hone his arguments. In the Diaries he was not engaged in work on which his reputation would rest.

Also, the elevation of the Diaries to a special place fails to distinguish between temporal and intellectual foundations. The notion that a work is foundational in *time* is to say that it is amongst the first contributions an author made to a recognizable intellectual structure. However, this is not the same thing as suggesting that it must be foundational in *importance* — i.e. central to the interpretation of the theorist's intellectual trajectory. Intellectual careers can be marked by distinct phases in which the writer significantly develops or abandons values present at the inception of their thought. When these shifts are detected, it is sensible to refer to different conceptual foundations, that is, the philosophical presuppositions that governed the theorist's works at different periods. It cannot be assumed that because Tawney gave a religious basis to his concepts from 1912–1914, that religious basis was immanent in the way he presented those concepts in his subsequent output. Such an assumption represents a conflation of temporal and intellectual foundations — a conflation that has to be proved by demonstrating a conceptual affinity between works over an unfolding period of time. But as we shall show, no such demonstration is feasible: our chronological analysis will demonstrate that Tawney's body of work cannot be viewed as an exemplification of the Diaries because he significantly departed from these early formulations. The transposition of the themes of the *Commonplace Book* onto a political project that lasted for a further four decades is too simplistic, because the distance travelled from these early musings in Tawney's subsequent works is too great to allow any over-identification of the Diaries with later publications.

There is strong evidence, therefore, that the published works offer the most authentic representation of Tawney's thought, and that it would be wrong to interpret them through the lens of the *Commonplace Book*. The mistaken assumption of continuity between the inchoate formulation of ideas in the Diaries and Tawney's subsequent works leads to a distorted analysis, imbuing the *Commonplace Book* with an importance it does not possess. In our analysis, the Diaries are extracted from the integral thesis, allowing them to stand alone to see them in their own light, unclouded by reference to the sanctioned works.

We begin with an account of the *Commonplace Book*, which although it does not constitute the key to Tawney's subsequent political thought, does provide an insight into his early thinking on the subject. Having established the formulations of the Diaries in Chapter 2, successive chapters examine the published works, showing that Tawney's discussion of political thought is characterized by significant changes that expose the weaknesses of the orthodox conceptual approach. The positive benefit of adopting a chronological approach is apparent when the changes in Tawney's political concepts are analysed.

Chapter Two

The Pre-First World War Unpublished Writings

The Commonplace Book (The Diaries, 1912–1914) and The New Leviathan (1910–1914)

2.1 Introduction

In this chapter, the ideas expressed in two documents not published by Tawney are examined for the light they throw on his early views on political thought — the *Commonplace Book* or Diaries, which were published posthumously in 1972; and *The New Leviathan*, which was never published. There are close links between the two documents, in that they share a religious emphasis in sketching out a general philosophy of life; they focus on political concepts; and they avoid making specific political prescriptions. But there is one difference — whereas in the Diaries, Tawney discusses rights entirely in the conservative context of duties, in *The New Leviathan* he puts forward a radical notion of natural rights.

2.2 The *Commonplace Book* (the Diaries, 1912–1914)

We do not have to accept the idea advanced by Winter, like Wright, that the Diaries provide the key to Tawney's published work (if only in an 'embryonic form' (Winter, 1972: XIII), to recognize that they convey the profound importance of Christianity to Tawney personally. In this chapter, we explore the Christian basis of the Diaries, not as the foundation stone of Tawney's subsequent political theory, but as the point of departure from which that theory was constructed.

2.2.1 Religion

Significantly, the religious basis of Tawney's early thought is largely taken for granted by him, rather than argued. For example, the existence of God is a given—a 'commonplace':

> God exists. That fact, in my view, is a fact of experience, by which I mean that consciousness of contact with a personality, or with a source of thought and emotion, is a fact of direct experience infinitely more immediate than reflection on an absent but existing person, and analogous to the consciousness of the presence of a person in the same room as oneself, whom one is not a[t] the moment looking at, and with whom one communicates nonetheless easily on that account. But this is a commonplace. (Tawney, 1972: 78)

Tawney's faith in God is not based on 'rationalist' arguments. The rational explanations that the order and interdependence of existence require an intelligent creative force, or that reality entails a first cause which cannot itself be the product of a previous cause, are eschewed in favour of a form of mystical intuition. This acceptance of the existence of God as a matter of faith rather than reason raises two questions: first, when and how did this strongly introspective faith emerge in Tawney's mind? Second, given the highly personal nature of his faith, why did Tawney assume that others should accept the existence of God and the associated doctrines, as his reference to the 'commonplace' suggests?

On the first point, commentators have assumed that Tawney's experiences as an undergraduate at Oxford were important in determining his Christian faith. This is given credence by the reputed influence of T.H. Green's Christian Idealism in the university, and the fact that Tawney's circle of acquaintances included clergymen such as Charles Gore. Both Greenleaf and Carter emphasize Gore's influence, the former referring to 'Gore who had been a student of TH Green and whose notion of a socially conscious Christianity became the guiding theme of Tawney's practical and intellectual career' (Greenleaf, 1983: 440; *cf.* Carter, 2003: 168–171). Carter adds that Tawney was not merely a passive depository for Christian idealism, but reciprocally influenced Gore, who quoted him in several of his works.

However, in his Diary, Tawney makes a statement that indicates that the above assumption has to be treated with care. He states that, as a university student, he did not view Christianity in a particularly favourable light: 'One of the things which strikes me as I grow older is the extraordinary truth of the religious dogmas at which, as an undergraduate, I used to laugh' (Tawney, 1972: 15). This statement suggests that the Christianity to which Tawney was exposed as an undergraduate may have had a longer gestation period than is normally recognized, only emerging to the fore during his stay at Toynbee Hall. Accepting that a precise time period cannot be identified as marking his conversion, discovering why Tawney came to accept these 'truths' is problematic. However, given Tawney's intuitive, rather than scriptural, grasp of Christianity, it is likely that his acceptance was based on his unfolding life experiences in the historical context in which he lived.

On the second question of why Tawney should assume that others would share his deeply introspective faith, a hint to the answer is apparent in his statement that his intuitive grasp of God is 'commonplace'. A thread running through the Diaries is the conviction that Man, as a spiritual being, is naturally inclined towards religious values. For instance, this conviction is shown by Tawney's claim that the revolutionary ire of the working classes is generated by the industrial system's disregard for the 'immaterial graces and pieties' in favour of a crude utilitarianism (Tawney, 1972: 14). For Tawney, right conduct can only be determined by a 'transcendental, religious, or mystical' standard (Tawney, 1972: 64). Such a principle condemns any injustice, regardless of utilitarian benefits, because of the spiritual value of every human personality. Tawney suggests that knowledge of what is right and wrong resides within each of us (Tawney, 1972: 31), and it does so as a product of shared experience:

> This knowledge is, I would urge, the common property of Christian nations. If it is asked, on what is this based, I answer that it is based on the experience of life in all the principal nations of Western Europe, and that its validity is shown by the fact that when these propositions are stated in a general form, nobody in practice would venture to deny them. (Tawney, 1972: 31)

Tawney thus presents a conception of morality which is indelibly connected with the shared experience of Christian norms. Religious conceptions of conduct are so bound up with our historical legacy that their acceptance and adoption is habitual. Tawney does not, however, embrace the Burkean notion that customary beliefs are right by virtue of their persistence: he argues that the ultimate validity of religious values rests with their origin in God as well as the social consequences of not following them (Tawney, 1972: 31). The cultural imperialism implicit in this commitment ignores the impact that non-Christian religions and secular doctrines have had on notions of right conduct. For Tawney, ethics is inextricably linked with Christian principles.

This leads us to the three broad moral principles which, Tawney believes, are the common property of Christian nations, and therefore would not cause dissent (Tawney, 1972: 31): all individuals should be concerned with the consequences of their actions for others; it is forbidden to engage in deception to obtain pecuniary gain; and it is wrong to exploit the weakness of an individual to wring out terms to which the person would not submit as a free agent. These principles raise three issues. First, they are not so exclusively Christian as to preclude non-Christians or even atheists from embracing them. Second, a great deal of room is left by Tawney for the interpretation of these principles. A broad spectrum of secular, religious and political groupings could sincerely approve of these values, but apply them in very different ways. The Tawney of the *Commonplace Book* establishes firm principles, but does not consider the practical effects of their application. Third, given the wide range of moral instructions contained in the Christian religion, the question arises; 'Why highlight these three?' One possibility is that Tawney felt that these were an effective summary of the mass of religious precepts. Another option is that Tawney has selected them with a view to condemn the market society of which he disapproves. While the first principle could be credibly applied to a range of situations, the latter two principles seem tailored to criticizing capitalism. The specific mention of pecuniary gain and the unfair terms imposed on someone in a weak position are themes that Tawney vigorously pursues in his condemnation of industrial society when he discusses the reduction of humans to economic tools (Tawney, 1972: 6; 14; 22; 33; 38). It is possible, therefore, that Tawney's social commentary is not an abstract digest of religious dogma, but that the reverse is true — social conditions are helping to structure the elements of Christianity he chooses to emphasize. Significantly, when Tawney later analyses the pre-capitalist Christian tradition, he argues that its decline was not due to its lack of exegetic coherence, but to its failure to adapt to changed circumstances. As Wright cogently argues, Tawney 'was a moralist certainly, but also a robustly practical one' (Wright, 1987: 46).

2.2.2 Ethical community

In the Diaries, Tawney's vision of an ethical community is painted in both negative and positive terms. Negatively, he condemns contemporary society for failing to live up to the standards of Christian morality, and he is deeply pessimistic about the effectiveness of politics in bringing about moral improvement:

> Modern politics are concerned with the manipulation of forces and interest. Modern society is sick through the absence of a moral ideal. To try to cure this by politics is like make [sic.] surgical experiment on a man who is dying of starvation or who is poisoned by foul air. (Tawney, 1972: 9)

The corrupting influence of the false philosophy has infected politics to the extent that its concerns are confined to the technocratic management of economic affairs, rather than the fundamental moral principles that govern a community. The grubby business of reconciling divergent interests, building alliances and forging com-

promises is symptomatic of, rather than a cure for, the moral malaise that scars modern society. It is as if the practice of politics
denies it the purity which is necessary to restore moral health to
society. This pessimism in relation to political agency raises profound questions about the viability of Tawney's moral crusade. If
the state, with its huge legislative authority and power, is itself
enthralled by materialism, then what hope exists for the crafting of
a moral community? Perhaps Tawney's enterprise could progress if
it can identify which groups or factors are responsible for the malaise. The Marxist position of identifying the bourgeoisie as the
oppressor, and casting the revolutionary proletariat as the universal class that will resolve all historical antagonisms, was one possible answer. However, Tawney, despite his outrage at the appalling
treatment of the working classes, does not support a class-based
solution, because he believes that everyone is to blame for the
predicament:

> It is all of us. We see no wrong in taking dividends which are
> wrung out of the oppression of other people. Above all — and it
> all comes back to this — we see no wrong in using other people
> not as human *personalities*, but as *tools*, not as *ends* but as *means*.
> (Tawney, 1972: 13)

The bogus principles that operate in British society are not the
imposition of a self-seeking cabal, nor are they the products of a
vast ideological structure; they are nourished by the ethical miscon-
ceptions of the whole population. This notion of the moral fallibility
of Man is particularly evident in Tawney's memorable embrace of
the doctrine of original sin; the idea that Man's nature is eternally
blemished by the misdemeanour committed in the Garden of Eden:
'what goodness we have reached is a house built on piles driven
into black slime and always slipping down into it unless we are
building day and night' (Tawney, 1972: 15).

However, Tawney's notion that the wretched state of society
reflects the general failure of humanity to grasp the errors of its
ways does not seem to cohere with either his insistence that we all
know certain forms of conduct to be wrong because of our common
Christian inheritance, or his claim that the deleterious consequences of not following Christian precepts reinforces their veracity. Moreover, if political institutions and the great mass of the

population accept the vile practices of the existing system, how can there ever be a moral renaissance?

In a more positive and optimistic vein, Tawney delves back into the past to show that an ethical community can be established:

> [T]here are golden moments in the life of mankind when national aims seem to be bent for some noble purpose, and men live at peace in the harmony which springs from the possession of a common moral ideal. (Tawney, 1972: 17)

The present discontent should not, therefore, be viewed as an intrinsic part of the human condition; rather it is historically specific, related to the prevalence of a false philosophy. However, even if history provides us with examples of societies that were animated by a shared ethical ideal, this does not provide a compelling reason for believing that this benign state can be re-created. Tawney's optimism is particularly striking given the turbulent context in which he was writing. The years directly before the First World War were characterized in Britain by discord and a high degree of social unrest, described by the historian, Robert Rhodes James (1978: 260), as 'a period of fever, of violence, and of extreme tension'. Declining economic conditions, together with the dissemination of syndicalist propaganda, with its advocacy of workers assuming control of their factories, were perceived to be radicalizing the trade union movement, who responded with large-scale industrial unrest. The suffragettes were pursuing a campaign of civil disobedience comprising street protests, the public haranguing of ministers and hunger strikes; the vociferousness of the movement was aptly captured by Christabel Pankhurst's manifesto *Broken Windows* (1912): 'Our very definite purpose is to create an intolerable situation for the Government, and, if need be, for the public as a whole' (Pankhurst, cited in Raeburn, 1974: 170). Compounding this, Parliament, which was evenly balanced between government and opposition, was witnessing uproarious scenes over the 'Irish Question'. At one point, the Conservative leader, Bonar Law, appeared to advocate that Protestants take actions outside parliamentary democratic processes (Webb, 1978: 470–473).

Nevertheless, despite the fractious nature of pre-war Britain, Tawney displayed optimism in relation to achieving moral unity: 'It ought to be possible to place certain principles of social and economic conduct outside the sphere of party politics, as matters agreed upon by the conscience of the nation' (Tawney, 1972: 50). So notwithstanding profound contemporary political divisions and their often explosive manifestations, Tawney can still see grounds for value consensus. What is required is a principle that both transcends, and operates within, society. Drawing on the ethical stance of the *Commonplace Book*, Tawney believes that religion can perform this unique role. The transcendental nature of religion ensures that it stands above differences of class and wealth and therefore can act as an objective principle of unification (Tawney, 1972: 43). Tawney's assessment of Christianity as the common property of the nation underlies this sentiment: his belief that peace comes when the external arrangements of society 'correspond with their subjective ideas of justice', indicates that Tawney is appealing to the same spiritual intuition that characterizes his belief in God (Tawney, 1972: 70). But individual reflection is not sufficient; an institutional dynamic is necessary, and this takes the form of a church independent of the state:

> Man's spiritual nature needs an outward organisation as well as his material one. Therefore there must be a Church as well as a State. But the church must not be above the state, not because it is too bad but because it is too good, not because it is too weak, but because it is too strong... The ancient question whether church is to be above state or state is to be above church, finds its solution in a free church refusing the temporalities for the sake of the spiritualities. (Tawney, 1972: 71)

So Tawney does not see church and state as inherently antagonistic but as two different organizations with two different spheres — the temporal and the spiritual — though the spiritual nature of the Church's mission gives it an elevated status superior to that of the state because of its commitment to the more edifying aspects of existence. However, beyond the vague notion that it attends to spiritual matters, the precise role of the church within society is not made clear. Perhaps the fundamental moral realignment that Tawney suggests as the key to a harmonious society will require the church to formally immerse itself in the polluted temporal sphere. Or, perhaps, given Tawney's notion of the power of the streetcorner preacher, its spiritual persuasiveness will informally spill over into political practice. But either way, he leaves unanswered the question, how can the Church bring about the moral transformation of society without getting itself sullied in the murky world of politics? Moreover, given the Church's role in exposing the moral failings of capitalist society, the separation of church and state in their different areas of operation looks tenuous. If the Church engaged in temporal matters, not only would its purity be threatened, but also it would come into direct conflict with the state. Not for the first, or last, time, Tawney's position seems lacking in coherence.

2.2.3 Political concepts

In the *Commonplace Book*, Tawney highlights four political concepts — equality; liberty; rights; and duties. Although his account is not rigorous, it does indicate his early thoughts on these concepts — thoughts which were to change significantly away from their Christian foundations in Tawney's later published work.

EQUALITY

Tawney's sketches of equality in the diaries are heavily influenced by his commitment to Christianity. This is demonstrated in both his valuation of human beings, and his strong endorsement of asceticism. The first is highlighted by Tawney's aphorism that 'In order to believe in human equality, it is necessary to believe in God' (Tawney, 1972: 53). The concept of equality is for Tawney incomprehensible without the Christian notion of the equal valuation of all human beings. In other words, it is only the belief in God that provides the basis for the equal value of all: secular concepts of egalitarianism are fundamentally flawed. Without the Christian premise of the common fatherhood of God, the notion of human equality is meaningless. The basis of this claim is the Christian doctrine that as creatures of God, all individuals have an equal value. A denial of God's existence encourages a belief in inequality, allowing some humans to be reduced to mere tools, instrumental to the self-interest of others (Tawney, 1972: 54). Despite our different attributes, skills and intelligence we are united by our common ancestry in the Almighty, and to this conviction of divine origins is added the notion that humans have an 'identity of nature' (Tawney, 1972: 55). God's infinite greatness puts into perspective our shared inferiority, and exposes the nonsense of erecting barriers between members of the human family. Without the acceptance of an omnipotent God, humans 'invent or emphasise distinctions', allowing the mass of men to be reduced to means, rather than ends (Tawney, 1972: 54). However, Tawney's emphatic statement that the equal valuation of humans is dependent on a belief in God is exclusionary. It represents a dogmatic insistence that secular modes of thought are incapable of justifying the equal value of human beings.

The second feature of the concept of equality enunciated by Tawney in the Diaries is religious asceticism. For the early Tawney, material equality is not as important as mental equality. What matters is that people are not prevented by poverty from being able to do what is necessary to live a decent life. Tawney saw little connection between material abundance and the good society (Tawney, 1972: 17; 19). Indeed, he reasons that history provides examples of societies which have been materially impoverished, but generally content. This reflects his conviction that a satisfying existence depends on individuals being able to attain self-respect and self-reliance rather than material affluence. A lack of money *per se* does not undermine a person's self-esteem; rather it is the feeling that the conditions of an individual's life are beyond their control, determined by the will of another. Poverty is wrong to the extent that it reduces humans to this vulnerable position. A condition of poverty that allowed individuals to make the most of their talents and lead a spiritually fulfilling life, would not be objectionable to Tawney.

However, in the industrial age it seems that poverty has precisely the effect of limiting citizen's self-reliance, so what is the solution? Tawney is not proposing a return to the benign poverty that he claimed existed during the Middle Ages; nor does he use the biblical parable of the camel and the eye of the needle to praise the edifying effect of want. Tawney's solution, as far as he has formulated one at this stage, is to transfer the focus from economic problems to moral evaluations. There is a need to 'conquer poverty by despising riches' — a notion that would continue to feature in Tawney's later works (Tawney, 1972: 62). Rather than continuing to worship wealth and believe that ever-greater accumulation can solve our predicament, it is necessary to embrace a new philosophy that subordinates materialism to spiritual values:

> [T]he springs of happiness and contentment are to be found not in the power of men to satisfy wants, but in the power of man to regard his position in society and that of his fellows with moral approval or satisfaction. (Tawney, 1972: 19)

Thus at this stage of his life, Tawney is thinking of equality more in moral terms than in material terms: true equality is to be achieved less by economic redistribution than by cognitive reorientation. However, in this discussion of equality, Tawney does not make clear the precise nature of the duties that humans owe to one and other; nor does he enunciate any particular form of egalitarianism, such as equality of opportunity or equality of outcome. Only one egalitarian principle is put forward—the equal right to an education. Tawney insists that the acquisition of knowledge should be a universal entitlement:

> [T]hink of knowledge, like religion, as transcending all differences of class and wealth; and that in the eye of learning, as in the eyes of God, all men are equal, because all are infinitely small. To sell education for money is the next thing to selling the gifts of God for money. (Tawney, 1972: 43)

Tawney thus imbues education with a sacramental significance, condemning its current confinement to the privileged, and commending its availability to the whole population. So while Tawney characteristically avoids a prescription, he enunciates a principle that has profound policy implications. On this reading, private education is not merely socially unacceptable, it borders on institutionalized blasphemy.

LIBERTY

Tawney's concept of liberty is an amalgam of two elements: power and individual development. Power, which is the means, is the capacity to 'control the condition of one's own life' (Tawney, 1972: 22). Individual development is the end, for which power is necessary. A pervasive theme throughout the Diaries is the tendency of industrial society to create a dependency relationship between the rich and the poor, with the latter wholly dependent on the former for the maintenance of their existence. This lack of liberty is the product of economic arrangements that ensure that the attainment of mere sustenance requires the compliance of the workers with the capitalist system. Workers are reduced to mere instruments of mass production, sacrificing their faculties and skills to serve the needs of the system. This condition of economic enslavement has profound psychological implications, with hopelessness, irresponsibility and recklessness the prominent features of working class life (Tawney, 1972: 34). Without the capacity for self-direction, the individual personality is stifled, unable to express its many contours or develop to its full potential. While there are some spiritual elements in this understanding of liberty, it is the material implications that are accorded greater prominence; Tawney embraces liberty as a social concept which is shaped by prevailing economic circumstances.

Although the arguments of the *Commonplace Book* are not sufficiently developed to draw firm conclusions about the policy implications of Tawney's views on liberty, he does make an important distinction between constitutional liberty and economic liberty, arguing that England led the way in securing the former, yet at the expense of endangering the latter:

> In the 17th century England upheld constitutional liberty when all other nations were passing under absolutism — England is the last country that hath a Parliament. Let it not perish now — can we not teach the world the meaning of economic liberty in the 20th? We owe it to the world to try. For we led it into the moral labyrinth of capitalist industry. (Tawney, 1972: 17)

Tawney argues that Britain's exceptional historical development provides it with a sense of mission; it needs to continue to propagate the fundamental constitutional or political freedoms that it produced, and to begin to atone for the economic enslavement that accompanies capitalism. This indicates that Tawney's campaign for economic liberty was to be fought within the historical hallmarks of British constitutionalism and the rule of law:

> The labour movement... really stands more than any other movement, for freedom today. What it demands is that men should not live their lives at the will of a master. The way in which it seeks to attain it is the old English way of the rule of

> law, that there shall be a settled constitution, that thousands
> shall not be dependent on the caprices of a few, like slaves, but
> that they shall have a voice in settling the conditions under
> which they may live. This is what the appeal to the State, the
> Socialism which frightens so many good souls, really means.
> (Tawney, 1972: 47)

England has historically secured the liberty of its subjects within
the political realm, and in the modern age, the test of freedom needs
to be applied to an economic sphere in which power is derived from
ownership. Capitalist society has emasculated the broad mass of
the population, with employees hopelessly dependent on the
owner merely to obtain a basic subsistence. The traditional English
concern with political freedom does not lead Tawney to embrace
the classical liberal economic notion in which liberty is preserved
by allowing economic actors free rein to pursue their interests.
Rather it necessitates a radical dispersal of power with the transfer
of property rights; the embrace of a principle of service; and the liberation of the proletariat from a mere productive tool to a sacred,
holistic human being. But all this will be secured by settled constitutional means. At this early stage in his political development,
Tawney is not overtly interested either in a radical overhaul of the
political sphere, or in proposals to construct a democracy more
expressive of the will of the people, although there is an early mention of guild socialism, and a concern to combat a sterile collectivism (Tawney, 1972: 79).

Tawney's notion of English exceptionalism does not merely signal
the acceptance of liberal constitutional norms, but also underlines
the strong nationalist dynamic that operates in the *Commonplace
Book*. By suggesting that there is a unique relationship between Britain and the development of political liberty, and stressing that this
should serve as an exemplar for other countries to follow, Tawney
is privileging national experience and asserting the superiority of
the country's political arrangements.

RIGHTS AND DUTIES

There is a strong notion of rights in the above analyses of equality
and liberty. Tawney is asserting the spiritual right to equality
before God; the constitutional right to political liberty; and the

moral right to economic liberty. However, Tawney's understanding of rights is inextricably bound up with a powerful sense of duty. The close relationship between rights and duties is encapsulated in Tawney's spiritual notion of the 'freedom to serve':

> One knows from one's inner experience, that spiritual well-being consists in finding one's work and doing it. This involves subordination, and therefore subordination is of the essence of a good society. What we all want is freedom to serve; for 'God and the king have not given the poor living we have, but to do service[s] therefore among our neighbours abroad'. In this idea, 'freedom to serve', rights and duties are reconciled. (Tawney, 1972: 57)

This idea of subordination reflects the religious austerity that characterizes much of the Diaries. Luxuries and agencies of frivolous enjoyment are condemned as distractions from social obligations, and Tawney denies a linkage between societal contentment and material abundance. In the *Commonplace Book*, Tawney claims that modern economic growth has not been accompanied by greater contentment, and he contrasts the general air of dissatisfaction in modern materialist society with the benign poverty of the Middle Ages in which there was widespread material deprivation, but a general moral satisfaction with social conditions, leading him to conclude that 'a satisfying social system is very largely independent of the material environment' (Tawney, 1972: 18–19).

The reference to spiritual well-being demonstrates that the need to serve is ingrained in humans as God's creatures. The failure to meet obligations is not a trivial affair, which leads to mild regret, but a fundamental failure that damages the individual's concept of selfhood. The deep yearning for freedom which all men possess is not related to egotistical self-expression, still less to hedonism; rather it is based on the need to meet obligations. Tawney states that 'the way of freedom is also the way of duty' (Tawney, 1972: 57). Rights exist to meet obligations to our family and the creation of the good society, not to allow a sphere in which we can engage in activities which are undertaken with the sole objective of selfish pleasure. This is not to say that Tawney was opposed to self-affirmation; rather he believed that the individual attained fulfilment precisely in the act of subordination. Tawney's belief that the essence of freedom is subordination places him amongst the advocates of positive liberty, for whom freedom is not an ultimate value that can be justified in its own terms, but a means to the end of duty. But it also exposes him to the criticism that if the individual is subsumed within the collective, finding expression and fulfilment only in terms of his/her contribution to a society pervaded with obligations, what real freedom does this entail? Tawney evidently found no reason to acknowledge, let alone explore, the potentially negative implications for freedom in a duty-based society.

Tawney's account of political concepts in the Diaries is thus an eclectic concoction. Equality and liberty are depicted by him in terms of individual worth and empowerment, but in his discussion of rights and duties it becomes apparent that humans are subordinated to an ethical community founded on Christian norms. Tawney believed that he was humanizing freedom by allowing individuals to meet their domestic duties and enabling them to take a more active role in economic and political life. But even if we concede that Tawney crafts liberty with a human face, the expression on that face is stern.

2.3 *The New Leviathan* (1910–1914)

Contained in the Tawney archive, *The New Leviathan* is a set of notes that were intended to contribute to a book that was subsequently abandoned. It is a curt, crisp discussion that invokes grand themes with a directness that lacks the elegant digressions and polished prose of the published works. The dating of these handwritten fragments is a matter for conjecture, but in the Tawney archive catalogue it is reckoned that they were produced during the period 1910–14. There are some striking similarities between the formulations of *The New Leviathan* and the Diaries. For example, both have a religious emphasis, both focus on political concepts, and both craft a general philosophy of life rather than propose concrete measures. But there is one major contrast between them: unlike the Diaries,

The New Leviathan contains a concept of natural rights. The following analysis focuses on these two themes of the work: first, its strong affinity with the *Commonplace Book*, particularly in its religious foundation; and second, its comments on natural rights, which offer a contrast not only to the Diaries, but also to Tawney's subsequent views on the subject.

2.3.1 Affinities with the Commonplace Book

The New Leviathan is a more academically-inclined version of the Diaries—less an introspective rumination than an effort to present some of the themes of the *Commonplace Book* in a more coherent form. As in the Diaries, Tawney pens in *The New Leviathan* an assault on contemporary materialism. Just as a concern with the prevalence of false philosophy peppers the Diaries' entries, so it is a dominant theme of *The New Leviathan* that Britain is suffering from a deficient moral ethos. Tawney attacks the widespread conviction that modern problems require an economic solution, when society lacks a comprehensive ethical ideal (Tawney, 1910–14: 1). Tawney deprecates the dominant ethos of modern society with its framework fitted to preserving the status quo, which prefers tinkering with social reform to boost efficiency, rather than undertaking a fundamental moral enquiry, grounded in an assessment of essential humanity (Tawney, 1910–14: 2; 10; 13). Tawney castigates social critics for treating the deformities of society as a set of intellectual problems that can be rectified by applying scientific techniques. Such critics fail to recognize that the current malaise is not the product of technical flaws, but is essentially a 'moral problem involving the alleviation of personal faults, ideals, and conduct' (Tawney, 1910–14: 13). In common with the Diaries, Tawney does not view the existing system as an elitist imposition on an emasculated majority; rather all share some personal responsibility for the perpetuation of the system which appeals to the baser instincts rather than to ethical principles. This false philosophy is apparent in the predominance of a utilitarianism that 'substitutes the canon of convenience for a canon of right and wrong', with the acceptance of an 'ethics' as a set of pliable principles crafted in terms of contingencies, rather than a morality grounded in divine doctrine (Tawney,

1910–14: 2). The conceptual affinities between this approach and that contained in the Diaries is striking, particularly when Tawney asserts that the social reformist approach to problems denies 'that there is, or is needed, any supernatural sanction for the validity of human methods of procedure and conduct' (Tawney, 1910–14: 2):

> The unstated assumption of the existing order of institutions and ideas is that society belongs to a purely human or 'natural' order; that there are no divine or absolute principles or laws laying down the lines upon which man is to seek well-being. Humans arrangements are, therefore, regarded as a matter of convenience, more or less expediency, more or less happiness… it is not thought to say 'Man is of such and such a nature, with such and such obligations to God, to enforce such and such rights and duties'. (Tawney, 1910–14: 3)

Moreover, as in the Diaries, Tawney affirms in *The New Leviathan* that the moral ideal lacking in contemporary society is Christianity, and that the Church has an important role to play in bringing about the necessary moral transformation. Tawney's call in *The New Leviathan* for the creation of the Good Society based on a 'fixed point principle' is absolutist and a-temporal: the same Christian conception that crowns the Diaries drives this work. Although Tawney is disparaging about the main mode of thought in contemporary society, he does not suggest that society is entirely bereft of goodness, but the little that remains is a historical hangover from Christianity rather than a secular doctrine (Tawney, 1910–14: 4; 11). The existence of God is the certainty from which all should unfold; the secular doctrine of social reform is merely propping up a society that is fatally flawed, incapable of delivering the edifying existence integral to Man's sacred significance. *The New Leviathan* thus remains within the parameters of the *Commonplace Book*, expressing a Christian exclusivity in which contemporary values and arrangements are criticized from a faith-based position. Tawney suggests that the people can be introduced to the 'point of view necessary to salvation' by asking them 'How and why do our current institutions and ideas fail to satisfy the deepest parts of human nature?' (Tawney, 1910–14: 4). The only answer to that question is that those institutions and ideas are not informed by the Christian religion, which is

the measure of man, his values and institutions, and the only body
of thought that can deliver justice.

As in the Diaries, where Tawney argues that Christianity
requires an institutional organization to assist its dissemination, so
in *The New Leviathan* he gives the Church a pivotal role in guiding
society toward enlightenment:

> If men accepted the leading light of the Christian Church, they
> would have a body of principles not only resting on authority
> (not the most important point) but setting out the main lines of
> a moral scheme of the universe, deducing man's duties and
> rights, freedom, responsibility, justice etc, from a definite con-
> ception of the nature of man and his relation to God. (Tawney,
> 1910–14: 4)

Ethical ideas are not sufficient in themselves, but require a representative, the Church. The Church has an interpretive function,
clarifying Christian precepts, showing how they impact on the values and structures of society that are normally placed in the political sphere. For Tawney, so-called 'political' values are derived from
a divine doctrine, and the Church is the proper body to flesh them
out and provide instruction on the legitimacy of their application in
a concrete setting. The Church thus has an implied, if not explicitly
stated, political function, reflecting Tawney's pessimism towards
the political system. *The New Leviathan* has the same aim as the Diaries, to create a Christian collective, with the Church occupying a
place of particular prominence. As in the Diaries, however, in *The
New Leviathan* Tawney is vague on how the Church should operate
to promote its values.

2.3.2 Natural rights

The second theme of *The New Leviathan* is Tawney's enunciation of
the doctrine of natural rights. Here he diverges from the *Commonplace Book*, where rights were seen only in close relation to duties. In
The New Leviathan, Tawney refers to rights as 'sacred and indefeasible', and attacks modern society for treating rights as matters of
concession, to be granted only when politically convenient. It is
wrong 'To regard human beings not as possessing rights qua
human being, which are sacred and indefeasible; but conceded... as

the convenience of the system may from time to time allow' (Tawney, 1910–14: 1). He claims that 'men feel they have natural rights that are logically prior to the organism' (Tawney, 1910–14: 5). Like Locke, Tawney derives these natural rights from God, asserting that as 'a child of God and heir of eternal life [man] has rights which are superior to the claims of the temporal order' (Tawney, 1910–14: 5–6). And although he criticizes the secular advocates of natural rights for omitting their supernatural origin, Tawney stresses that such exponents of the doctrine 'were not wrong in what they stated'; indeed, they were 'right in thinking that the individual had certain rights which are absolute' (Tawney, 1910–14: 5–6).

Whilst the unpublished status of *The New Leviathan* weakens its interpretive significance, it does demonstrate that Tawney engaged with the concept of natural rights, and contemplates using it in his political thought during the early stages of his intellectual career. In subsequent chapters, we will show how Tawney twice altered his position on rights: first, re-asserting their dependence on duties in *The Acquisitive Society*, and denigrating a social system that would operate in terms of absolute rights; and second, in the essays of the forties and fifties, returning to abstract rights as the basis for a decent society attempting the delivery of justice. Our chronological approach allows a more accurate depiction of Tawney's position than does the essentialist approach of Carter (2003: 175), who asserts that Tawney 'rejected the notion of natural rights which had been common in the nineteenth century', holding that 'all rights had to be put to the test of social justification; did they or did they not help fulfil the common good'. Terrill (1973: 169), although acknowledging (unlike Carter) Tawney's flirtation with natural rights, dismisses it as an aberration in his attempt to craft a cohesive Tawney theory of rights: 'Despite a note in "The New Leviathan" which may suggest the contrary, Tawney was not restoring the eighteenth-century idea of rights (in the same fragment he criticises the eighteenth century idea on the ground that it lacked a "supernatural reference")'. The picture we present is a good deal more complicated than either Carter or Terrill allow, and *The New Leviathan* plays a part in revealing Tawney's changing mindset.

2.4 Conclusion

This chapter has examined two works by Tawney, neither of which he himself published, to discover his early ideas on political thought. In the *Commonplace Book*, or Diaries (which was posthumously published), we found a strong statement of the religious foundation of Tawney's pre-First World War views on the English political and social system, expressed particularly in his denunciation of its largely secular, materialistic ethos, and in his proposal for a positive role for the Christian Church in the moral regeneration needed to bring about the restoration of an ethical community. We also found ideas on the political concepts of equality, liberty, and rights, which Tawney interprets within a strict code of Christian duty, though without providing details of their implications for public policy. In *The New Leviathan* (which was never published), we found considerable affinity with the Diaries, especially in emphasizing the religious basis of politics, and the important role of the Church in reforming it. There was, however, one important difference between the two works: in his account of rights in *The New Leviathan*, Tawney exchanges the constraints of duty for the absoluteness of natural rights, though still within a Christian framework.

These early works do not, however, support the essentialist interpretation of Tawney's political thought. They demonstrate that his early ideas are not systematically or rigorously argued: indeed, Tawney's discussion is often founded on unexamined assumptions, some of which are mutually contradictory, with little attempt to engage in argument. The sharp difference between the two works on the nature of rights – the duty-based account in the Diaries, contrasted with the natural rights-based account in *The New Leviathan* – indicates that there was not even consistency between Tawney's early works, let alone consistency between his early and late works. Moreover, there is little or no attempt by Tawney to flesh out the practical implications of the principles he enunciates in either of the two works. It is difficult to accept, therefore, that such works can be seen as authoritative conceptual contributions. This is not a criticism of *Tawney*, because his intention in these early pieces was not to produce a complete, closely argued political tract which could have a practical effect on policy: he was not addressing an audience, academic or political, but engaged in an introspective search for meaning. But it is a criticism of the *commentators* who bestow pre-eminent status on the *Commonplace Book* as an expression of the fundamentals of Tawney's political thought.

These two works do, however, provide us with an insight into the ideas which Tawney held before he developed his considered political theory. They constitute a launching pad for that theory, and we can evaluate his considered political theory partly as a journey away from these early ideas. As we will see in the next chapter, where we consider Tawney's published essays during the period 1913–1921, culminating in the publication of his first major work, *The Acquisitive Society*, this journey takes the form of gradually loosening the religious basis of his political thought.

Chapter Three

The Road to The Acquisitive Society (1913–1921)

3.1 Introduction

In this chapter, Tawney's political ideas in six works—five essays and a book—published during the period 1913–1921 are examined: *Poverty as an Industrial Problem* (1913); *The Attack* (1916); *Some Reflections of a Soldier* (1916); *A National College of All Souls* (1917); *The Conditions of Economic Liberty* (1918); and *The Acquisitive Society* (1921). Most attention is paid to the book (the last work) because of its iconic status in the Tawney canon, but we show how the five essays reveal a gradual relinquishing of the religious coping of Tawney's political thought that was evident in the *Commonplace Book*. This shift culminates in *The Acquisitive Society*, where a predominantly secular critique of the ills of contemporary society is presented, though with the addition of a concluding section in which a religious coping is unexpectedly re-introduced, as though Tawney temporarily lost his nerve about cutting out the religious root from his political theory.

3.2 *Poverty as an Industrial Problem* (1913)

During the writing of the *Commonplace Book*, Tawney was appointed as the Director of the Ratan Tata Foundation. This organization, founded by an Indian businessman, was established to analyse the causes of poverty and to propose remedies. In his inaugural directorial lecture, entitled *Poverty as an Industrial Problem* (1913), Tawney applauded the growing maturity of research studies in viewing poverty not as a product of the frailties of the afflicted, but as a condition nourished by a particular form of social organization (Tawney, 1978: 117–123). Poverty could not be dismissed as the inevitable result of the defective individual; its causes must be sought in the structures of industrial arrangements. It is instructive to see how knowledge of the Diaries assists our interpretation of this lecture, which was written at the same time, because, in it, Tawney touches on themes that animated his private reflections, although his focus here is considerably narrower and more systematic. For instance, he rejects the cold logic of social Darwinism, arguing that the 'fittest' do not always survive: 'In the social strata where large properties are inherited, the fool and the genius have an equal chance of survival. Where sanitary conditions are such as to produce cholera, good stock and bad stock perish together' (Tawney, 1978: 125). Even if inherited qualities are pre-eminent in the make-up of the individual, it is only by establishing conditions conducive to the maintenance of everyone's life that allows us to differentiate between the 'undeserving' poor and those who are victims of circumstance.

It can be inferred from the views expressed in the Diaries that Tawney believed that the reformation of society would unlock the mass potential of the working classes and demonstrate the vacuity of social Darwinism. In line with this belief, towards the end of his inaugural lecture, Tawney declares that the Ratan Tata Foundation should investigate the effectiveness of existing welfare provision in alleviating poverty (Tawney, 1978: 127). In establishing this aim, Tawney led by example, conducting research into the operation of the minimum rates in the chain-making and tailoring industries, suggesting that the Liberal social welfare reforms had stimulated wage growth without substantially increasing unemployment (Tawney, 1915: 254).

Perhaps respectful of the purpose of the foundation to generate an empirical understanding of deprivation, Tawney's moral exhortations are kept to a minimum. However, in his opening remarks, he cannot resist referring to the 'social evils' which remain, not because 'we do not know what is wrong, but the fact that we prefer to continue doing what is wrong' (Tawney, 1978: 111). Given what we know of the *Commonplace Book*, the density of this comment is revealed, because it is expressive of Tawney's belief that morality is a product of our common Christian heritage. In this sense, a clear conceptual link is discernible between the two works, though it is notable that Tawney's argumentation is less emphatic in this lecture than in the Diaries.

Tawney's career came to an abrupt halt in 1914 with the onset of World War One. He refused to be seduced by pacifist nostrums or radical propaganda that depicted the struggle as a futile capitalist war, and he volunteered for service. Typically, he refused the officer posting to which his status entitled him and he joined up as a private, quickly rising to the rank of sergeant. He led a company in the Battle of the Somme and was fortunate to survive one of the most horrendous battles of the conflagration. In the early stages of combat he was shot in the chest and abdomen:

> What I felt was that I had been hit by a tremendous iron hammer, swung by a giant of inconceivable strength, and then twisted with a sickening sort of wrench so that my head and back banged to the ground, and my feet struggled as though they didn't belong to me. (Tawney, 1953: 18)

Tawney was left stranded in no man's land, while the fighting continued unabated. After he was rescued, Tawney was discharged on medical grounds and resumed his academic career. Tawney's personal experiences of war during 1914–16 had a profound impact on his thought, which needs to be understood to interpret accurately the evolution of his political theory. Significant for this purpose are four essays, two dealing with the war and the expectations created by it, and two which are amongst Tawney's first public efforts to craft a practical philosophy. First, we consider the war essays.

3.3 *The Attack* (1916);
Some Reflections of a Soldier (1916)

Soon after his discharge in 1916, Tawney published two articles in the *Nation*, entitled *The Attack* and *Some Reflections of a Soldier*, which were reissued in a book entitled *The Attack* (1953). The former provides an account of the Battle of the Somme, including Tawney's near-death experience, and the latter deals with the sense of dislocation that Tawney feels on confronting civilian life. Two contrasting points about human nature — one negative and the other positive — can be extracted from these essays. The negative point is that Tawney's experience of combat reinforces his conception of original sin. His embrace of the doctrine of original sin in the Diaries was essentially a regurgitation of the biblical conception, with little substantiation from Tawney's own experience at the time of writing. His subsequent exposure to war conflict gave Tawney's enunciation of the doctrine a profound personal sense of reality, as this passage from *The Attack* indicates:

> Most men, I suppose, have a Palaeolithic savage somewhere in them, a beast that occasionally shouts to be given a chance of showing his joyful cunning in destruction. I have, anyway... One's like a merry mischievous ape tearing up the image of God. (Tawney, 1953: 15–16)

The litany of the horrors Tawney witnessed, such as the hatred in the eyes of the injured comrades he had to abandon and his own atavistic pleasure in targeting the enemy, led him to confront directly the dark attributes that were part of his own nature, rather than to merely regurgitate a biblical platitude. It is striking that Tawney equivocates in generalizing these attributes to others bound up in the conflict. In the *Commonplace Book*, Tawney's introspective psychological deductions are often applied to others without any sense of discrimination. But in *The Attack*, Tawney is hesitant about extrapolating his thoughts to others, adding qualifications which make clear that these are his own personal perceptions. Nevertheless, Tawney's involvement in trench warfare gave his conviction of the destructive capacity of human nature a depth altogether lacking in the empty analogies of his pre-war sketches.

Tawney's adherence to the doctrine of original sin is transformed from a theoretical religious belief to a notion with a vivid experiential root. His discussion of his own conduct powerfully illustrates the inhuman forces that can be unleashed when the circumstances demand.

The positive point is that in *The Attack*, Tawney presents notions of human qualities that are far removed from the negativity about human nature portrayed in the Diaries. For instance, his exaltation of his comrades, with the perception that conflict has stimulated their idealism and delivered them to a higher phase of social consciousness, is in marked contrast to the dour and negative conception of humanity often depicted in the *Commonplace Book*. It is true that in the Diaries Tawney had expressed some positive views about humanity: his admiration for his working class students is undoubted, particularly as he often paraphrased their thoughts on modern society. However, the extreme conditions of World War One engendered a spirit of humanity far greater than anything expressed in the Diaries. In *Some Reflections of a Soldier*, for example, Tawney contrasts the propagandistic depiction of the typical British soldier carried by the press with the reality displayed in the theatre of war, where despite (or rather because of) their own horrendous suffering, British soldiers were able to see the enemy German soldiers as fellow victims:

> Do you expect us to hurt them or starve them? Do you not see that we regard these men who sat opposite us in the mud — 'square headed bastards,' as we called them — as the victims of the same catastrophe as ourselves, as our comrades in misery much more truly than you are? (Tawney, 1953: 25)

The notion of identity is applied here not between the soldiers and civilians of Britain, but between the combatants on opposite sides in the trenches. Tawney is suggesting that the British and German soldiers, because of their mutual experience of the barbarity of conflict, have formed an understanding that almost constitutes a community in suffering. Here is a former combatant chastising the home population and seeing a greater affinity between himself and the German enemy in the field than between himself and civilians in Britain. Indeed, Tawney is convinced that a profound chasm now exists between soldiers and civilians of Britain. Whereas, in the

Commonplace Book, Tawney sees class as the major division in society. The war, which was expected to create a culture of national
co-operation and harmony, has produced a new cleavage, with the
returning soldier alienated from the *mores* of the country he
defended. As Tawney puts it in *Some Reflections of a Soldier*,

> when, as has happened in the present war, men have taken up
> arms, not as a profession or because forced to do so by law, but
> under the influence of some emotion or principle, they tend to
> be ruled by the idea which compelled them to enlist long after it
> has yielded, amongst civilians, to some more fashionable nov-
> elty. (Tawney, 1953: 23)

In the Diaries, one of Tawney's most arresting passages referred to
the capacity of nations to attain a 'golden moment' of harmony in
which the population were animated and united by a common purpose. It is during these periods that progress may be made and
social evils may be extinguished. The pre-war sketches certainly
suggest that a movement for fundamental change is emerging
amongst the general context of materialist vice, as is evident in
Tawney's suggestion that the moralizing of street corner preachers
is beginning to penetrate popular consciousness. It is in this spirit
that Tawney's involvement in the First World War may be interpreted: not only was it a duty to defend a democracy against an
autocratic enemy, but it was also an opportunity to revitalize and
revolutionize the values of British society. However, the country to
which Tawney returned in 1916 has failed to capitalize on this
opportunity. Instead of seeing the war as a unifying force, civilians
at home have viewed the post-war period as an opportunity to
make profits, for which Tawney bitterly rebukes them in *Some
Reflections of a Soldier*:

> You speak lightly, you assume that we shall speak lightly, of
> things, emotions, states of mind, human relationships and
> affairs, which are solemn or terrible. You seem ashamed, as if
> they were a kind of weakness, of the ideas which sent us to
> France, and for which thousands of sons and lovers have died.
> You calculate the profits to be derived from 'War after the War',
> as though the unspeakable agonies of the Somme were an item
> in a commercial proposition. (Tawney, 1953: 21–22)

The tone of this passage is reflective of the whole essay, in which Tawney's thoughts are characterized by an overwhelming sense of betrayal. Those who served in the armed forces and experienced the destructive nature of war have returned with their ideals not merely preserved but reinforced, yet the principles for which they fought are not reflected in a society irredeemably driven by materialism. Tawney was appalled at the way in which British civilian society belittled the sacrifices made by soldiers, especially by its stereotypical image of the British Tommy, joyfully revelling in the carnage and slaughter of war:

> We are depicted as merry assassins, rejoicing in the opportunity of a 'scrap' in which we know that more than half our friends will be maimed or killed, careless of our own lives, exulting in the duty of turning human beings into lumps of disfigured clay, light-hearted as children who shoot at sparrows with a new air-gun and clap their hands when they fall, charmed from transient melancholy of childhood by a game of football or a packet of cigarettes. (Tawney, 1953: 25)

His outrage at the crude trivialization of conflict presented by politicians, carried by the newspapers, and imbibed by the common man, creates a sense of deep pessimism about the capacity of the country to face the tasks that will necessarily follow from the end of hostilities. Tawney believed that these fantastical accounts of war were 'an index of the temper in which you will approach the problems of peace' (Tawney, 1953: 24). For Tawney, the war was a crystallizing experience for all those who were directly involved; it is as if those who fought had attained a higher state of knowledge precisely because they have plumbed the depths of human existence. The path of the civilian population, immersed in the romantic fable of the purity of war fuelled by an intense hatred of the German enemy, has diverged from the path of the soldiers, disillusioned from extreme chauvinism by the harsh realities of combat, to form a major division in society — a moral gulf between civilian and soldier. The moral degradation of the civilian perception is graphically expressed by Tawney in a passage at the conclusion of *Some Reflections of a Soldier*:

> But it is not among those who have suffered most cruelly or whose comprehension of the tragedy is most profound that I

find hatred which appals. For in suffering, as in knowledge, there is something that transcends personal emotion and unites the soul to the suffering and wisdom of God. I find it rather among those who, having no outlet in suffering or in action, seem to discover in hatred the sensation of activity which they have missed elsewhere. They are to be pitied, for they also are seeking a union with their kind, though by a path on which it cannot be found. Nevertheless, the contagion of your spirit is deadly. Every inch that you yield to your baser selves, to hatred, to materialism which waits on spiritual exhaustion, is added to the deadly space across which the Army must drag itself to its goal and yours. You do not help yourselves, or your country, or your soldiers, by hating, but only by loving and striving to be more lovable. (Tawney, 1953: 27–28)

The idea of a civilian population consumed by hatred, poisoning the prospects for a more humane post-war society, reveals the spiritual dynamic that underlies the language used in the early part of the essay. Tawney contrasts soldiers as exalted through struggle with a profound sense of the need for peace, to civilians twisted by the contempt for the enemy that has been crafted and perpetuated by home front propaganda, and he issues a warning that the civilian mindset could triumph and create a country that nurtures the worst aspect of human nature. Indeed, although the moral emphasis in the essays is not as overtly Christian as in the Diaries, there is clearly a religious dynamic operating. This is most explicit in the notion that the soldiers united in suffering are closer to God and the values He embodies. It is difficult, therefore, to reject the essentialist interpretation that Tawney's faith emerged from the war unscathed. As Wright states, it 'produced no real dent in the structure of fundamental beliefs about man and society which he had put together before 1914, and his God had also survived intact' (Wright, 1987: 21). To this extent, then, the 1916 essays can legitimately be seen in terms of continuity with the Diaries.

At the conclusion of the *Commonplace Book*, Tawney links the domestic situation with the ensuing international turmoil, suggesting that the false materialistic values that were cultivated in peace-time had culminated in the catastrophe of war (Tawney, 1972: 83). The prosecution of this war, recognized as the product of vices propagated in pre-war economic arrangements, could be seen as an opportunity to scrutinize the social system and realize the ideals that Tawney identified in the pages of his Diaries. However, in the 1916 essays, this aspiration and, indeed, expectation that a new order would emerge, succumb to Tawney's pessimistic realization that the revolution had been thwarted.

Tawney resumed his academic career before the war ended, when the conflagration was still a major conditioning factor of his life. However, he was now beginning to view the war in a different context, not confined to imploring a shift in values, but advocating concrete measures to transform society. Tawney's writings during 1917 and 1918 embraced a new dimension that would pave the way for *The Acquisitive Society*.

3.4 *A National College of All Souls* (1917); *The Conditions of Economic Liberty* (1918)

In relation to the essays, *A National College of All Souls* (1917) and *The Conditions of Economic Liberty* (1918), commentators who adopt the essentialist interpretation of Tawney's political theory are not sufficiently scrupulous in drawing distinctions between the two pieces, and contrasting them with *The Attack* and *Some Reflections of a Soldier*. A close scrutiny of the four essays reveals a notable change in emphasis; in the two later essays, Tawney is much more optimistic about the prospects of social progress than in *The Attack* and *Some Reflections of a Soldier*. The two later essays are examined here both to establish their contribution to the practical character of Tawney's conception of politics, and to clarify his theoretical mindset before the publication of his seminal work, *The Acquisitive Society*.

The essay entitled *A National College of All Souls*, published only six months after Tawney's vitriolic *Some Reflections of a Soldier*, is to be distinguished from it by a more refined channelling of his thoughts into concrete proposals. For instance, in the later essay, Tawney develops a conception of debt to retuning soldiers, holding the nation to be morally obliged to recognize the sacrifices made by soldiers on its behalf by embracing educational reform. Tawney's thesis is strikingly simple: the school system mirrors our plutocratic society in which the wealthy receive an education 'lavish even to excess', while the remaining 80% of the population are given a rudimentary instruction that is grossly inadequate (Tawney, 1953: 34). Tawney calls for an educational system that is universal in scope and rich in depth—an appropriate monument to those who went to war to fight for a humane society. While Tawney is more prescriptive in this 1917 essay because he is dealing with reforming a specific institution, rather than merely appealing for a more peace-loving mood to soothe the nation as he does in *Some Reflections of a Soldier*, this call for educational expansion is accorded a symbolic significance in the struggle for a more spiritual existence:

> the sphere where the claims of personality are most clearly involved, and where what threatens them is most obviously the operation of materialistic motives, is the sphere of education. (Tawney, 1953: 34)

Tawney's concept of education embraces the idea that it is disinterested intellectual activity justified on its own terms, rather than an institution whose worth is determined by its contribution to the economy. Tawney's concern is primarily with self-development—that is individuals exercising their capabilities to the optimum level. Such an edifying experience should not be corroded by the spiritually impoverished conception of commercial expediency. If the endeavour of education cannot be protected from the clutch of industrialism, then society has surrendered to materialism. This primacy of education in the struggle against the materialistic values of industrialism is largely a derivative of Tawney's Christian beliefs. Employing Bacon's maxim, Tawney maintains that education should be pursued for 'the glory of God and the relief of man's estate', otherwise society is bereft of richness (Tawney, 1953: 32). This religious basis is an extension of the formulation in the *Commonplace Book*, where Tawney calls the purchase of education a form of sacrilege, and the general tenor of the article in its condemnation of private education gives no reason to suspect that Tawney's view has altered.

Another contrast between the All Souls essay and the earlier Reflections essay is that Tawney is more optimistic about the chances of an improvement in the national character. In the *A National College of All Souls* essay, after enunciating the notion familiar from the Diaries that an alteration in the national mentality is a pre-requisite for substantial structural change

> — It is the expression of the scale of values which rules in the minds of most individuals, and which, therefore, rules in the State. And we shall not make any serious progress until that scale is reversed, until the English people — and not merely 'the State' — is a little horrified at ignorance and vulgarity and stupidity. (Tawney, 1953: 31) —

Tawney gives the notion a more positive spin than in either the Diaries or *Some Reflections of a Soldier*, and his pervasive pessimism and sense of bitterness has been supplanted by a more positive view of the opportunity that exists to build anew. The war, by exhibiting some of the worst excesses of materialism and the highly destructive consequences of the German pursuit of dominance, made the case for change more compelling (Tawney, 1953: 33). This upbeat tone is missing from the earlier article, which focused more on the betrayed ideals of those who went into battle. Tawney's cynicism seems to have been modified, if not eradicated, and he is ready to develop a persuasive case for a concrete change.

This shift from Tawney's wartime pessimism is confirmed by the fourth so-called 'war essay' — *The Conditions of Economic Liberty* (1918) — which was initially published in the symposium, *Labour and Capital after the War*, and included in a posthumous collection of essays published in 1964, entitled *The Radical Tradition*. In this essay, Tawney is more explicit in making concrete proposals for the future development of Britain. These proposals are based on two assumptions: first, there will be no restoration of the old order because the moral and intellectual basis of the nation has been transformed (Tawney, 1964b: 97). The absolute certitude of Tawney's claim here strongly contrasts with his tentative attitude in *Some Reflections of a Soldier*. The suspicion expressed there that the British populace may have abandoned the high principles conducive to a civilized social settlement has been revised, and Tawney now views the tendencies unleashed by the conflagration to establish conditions that will define the social and political context in the post-war era. Any reassertion of materialism, with politicians believing that an increase in productivity will be sufficient to address existing problems, does not cohere with the national mood. A profound intellectual transformation has occurred in the national mentality because the notion that change can only be incremental has been contradicted by recent economic developments. The war, which led to the expansion of the state and the dilution of the market mechanism, demonstrated that change was the product of a 'collective act of will' (Tawney, 1964b: 99). The idea of the economy as a self-directed organism that operates independently of human will has been comprehensively discredited, and the possibility of altering arrangements in accordance with human motives has been convincingly demonstrated. The old methods are obsolete and a new course needs to be found.

This assumption reveals how far, in the course of two years, Tawney's position has changed. The educative value of the war was something that he previously confined to combatants, with the civilian population deceived by the spurious propaganda of the 'opinion formers'. The gaping cleavage that separated soldier and civilian has now been bridged by a collective acceptance of the values of enlightened reform:

> The question is not how to repair an industrial system dislocated by war. It is how to reform an industrial system which was felt to be incompatible with social freedom and justice in peace... Social Reconstruction either means Social Revolution, or it means nothing. (Tawney, 1964b: 98–99)

However, while this constitutes a departure from the narrative of *Some Reflections of a Soldier*, it does not represent an innovation in Tawney's thought; rather it signifies the resurrection of his pre-war position. The revolution, which he briefly thought had been betrayed, was merely deferred.

It is difficult to account for Tawney's sudden reassertion of revolutionary optimism. It may be tempting to interpret *Some Reflections of a Soldier* as an anomaly; a temporary deviation in the otherwise linear trajectory of Tawney's thought. However, the article stands as a self-conscious creation, voluntarily placed in the public arena and therefore in need of recognition in the Tawney canon. It could be interpreted as a work of provocation, with Tawney employing inflammatory language to provoke thought and ultimately convince his readers of the need for change. Certainly Tawney's emphasis on the capacity of ideas to influence social reality gives some credence to the notion that the essay could be a persuasive polemic, although given Tawney's revulsion towards the journalistic hyperbole used to depict the war, it is highly unlikely that he himself would resort to this form of expression. The most likely explanation is that the article is an emotional outpouring from a man who has witnessed the horrendous excesses of human suffering. Tawney's anger is the cathartic expression of frustration aimed at those who enjoyed the relative comfort of civilian life, blissfully unaware of the real horrors endured by the infantry and forgetful of the purposes of the sacrifice. Whatever the reason, it is sufficient to note the very different character of the two articles (*Some Reflections of a Soldier* and *The Conditions of Economic Liberty*), which demonstrates the problem of asserting their unity.

The second assumption on which Tawney bases his proposals for post-war development in *The Conditions of Economic Liberty* is his insistence that the war was not the cause of the problems that need to be solved; rather it was the 'lightning rod' that exposed them (Tawney, 1964b: 98). Tawney, revisiting the themes of the *Commonplace Book*, firmly attributes contemporary problems to the structure of economic relations that has developed over the course of four centuries. The war has simply uncovered these problems by exposing the fallacious assumptions that underpin British society (Tawney, 1964b: 98–100). For example, the domestic conflict between employer and employee, which threatened to deprive soldiers of coal and munitions, exposed a fundamental antagonism within the industrial system. The fact that internal economic arrangements could not operate effectively, even in a situation of this gravity, demonstrates the severity of the problems and shows that *laissez-faire* capitalism undermines the national interest. The excuse that the country does not have the material means to radically improve social conditions was belied by the massive sums used to commit the nation to war. Tawney estimates that military expenditure was greater than the amount annually spent on the provision of public health, education and housing put together, so government's protestations of financial paucity are not credible.

Taken together, these two assumptions represent a repudiation of the conservative consensus that the state should be economically passive, financially 'prudent' in limiting public expenditure and reluctant to initiate far-reaching change. While this shows Tawney's renewed optimism in identifying the war as a defining moment in the remodelling of society, this is a resurrection of his pre-war sentiment rather than an entirely new doctrine. Tawney does, however, go beyond his earlier position by being more explicit in outlining the nature of the new order (Tawney, 1964b: 105–112). He argues that capital must be stripped of its dominant role in society and subordinated to the needs of the community. This entails the creation of an economic structure that is fundamentally democratic, with workers and trade unions participating in roles which are currently the preserve of the management. Tawney envisages the establishment of National Councils of employers and workers, and workshop committees, which together will manage the economy, subjected to the limitations imposed by the wider community. Tawney is quite explicit that productive private property can only remain if it operates in a way that is consistent with the principles of social service and industrial democracy.

In bringing about this industrial democracy, the state could play an important part:

> If the conception of industry as a social function is to be effective, it must, then, be a spirit working within it not merely a body of rules imposed by an external authority. But, in the revolution needed to make the development of that spirit a possibility, the state can, if it pleases, play a considerable role. (Tawney, 1964b: 112)

This admission of a positive role for the state, albeit with the caveat 'if it pleases', marks an innovation in Tawney's thought, in that it contradicts the vociferous condemnation of the capacity of political intervention to effect moral renewal contained in the *Commonplace Book* (Tawney, 1972: 9). Tawney there characterized politics as morally impure, disbarring it from crafting a moral community: politics was intrinsically bound to the morally bankrupt system it helped to administer and, therefore, wholly incapable of extricating itself to create and sustain the new ethical philosophy necessary to establish the new order. Given the inherent flaws of political institutions, their operation was confined to the temporal sphere, while the spiritual realm, from which the unifying moral philosophy would emerge, was linked to Christianity and the Church. But in *The Conditions of Economic Liberty*, Tawney eschews this dichotomy, asserting the efficacy of political institutions in facilitating ethical arrangements:

> The right principle for the community to follow is simple, though its application may be complex. Though industrial reform cannot be imposed by the State, the State can, at least, emphasise the principle that industry and trade are a form of public service, and that the man who in time of peace plays on public necessities to amass a fortune... is morally on par with the merchant or manufacturer who holds his countrymen to ransom in the time of war. (Tawney, 1964b: 115)

Tawney had previously insisted on a division between state and church, maintaining that they operated in separate realms. His position now embraces the idea that the state can enter the spiritual realm to encourage forms of behaviour which are morally legitimate (Tawney, 1964b: 113–115). The state can perform this function by creating a framework which ensures that industry operates with greater transparency, obliging economic units to publish accounts for public scrutiny to guarantee that prices reflect costs, rather than to profiteer. The state should actively encourage the formation of enterprises which embody the enlightened values of social service, and discourage those organizations that remain committed to exploitative modes of organization. Tawney does not specify what form this discouragement will take, but given his suggestion that incomes which are not derived from socially useful activities should be subjected to special taxation, and his reluctance to propose coercion to compel companies to conform to these arrangements, it would seem that he favours an enabling, rather than a directorial, conception of state action.

Although Tawney's reappraisal of the role of the state, and with it his conception of political agency, does not mean he has abandoned the notion expressed in the Diaries that the persuasiveness of ideas is the main causal dynamic in social systems, his new position does represent a breach with the Christian exclusivity contained in the *Commonplace Book*. He has certainly moved from a position in which the state, enmeshed in a decadent structure of short-term expediency, is unable to provide edifying organizational ideals, to one in which the state has the capacity to extricate itself from the pervasive materialism and perform a positive role in the creation of an ethical community. The secular state has now been accorded a relative autonomy from the murky materialism that characterizes capitalism, and it is both philosophically and practically capable of contributing to the progressive revolution.

However, the source of the ethical ideals which must animate the state lies outside it. Despite Tawney's more benign view of the state, it does not contradict his argument in the *Commonplace Book* that parliament only has creative force when it can apply a body of ideas that exists outside itself (Tawney, 1972: 76). The difference is that this external source of social morality is no longer the Church, but the people. Tawney concludes *The Conditions of Economic Liberty* by stating that the responsibility for the introduction and consolidation of enlightened reform ultimately resides with the populace. While recognizing the possibility that the old order could reassert itself, Tawney is confident that the wartime spirit in the minds of the people will combat any lurch back to destructive materialism. Men energized by the defence of liberty will protect the vision of an enriched democracy that can be expanded into the economic sphere:

> It is possible that the pathetic instinct to demand payment for privilege, as though it were a kind of service, will re-emerge jaunty and unrepentant out of the sea of blood and tears in which it has been temporarily submerged, and that in a world where not a few have given all, there may still be classes and individuals whose ideal is not to give but to take. Such claims, if they are made, may be regarded with pity, but without apprehension. Men who have endured the rigors of war in order to make the world safe for democracy, will find ways of overcoming the social forces and institutions which threaten that cause in time of peace. (Tawney, 1964b: 116–117)

The Conditions of Economic Liberty, therefore, represents a positive reassertion of the potential for fundamental change, with a population educated by the rigours of war and a state structure capable of assisting progress. Tawney's reappraisal of the state as not inherently ensnared by materialist capitalist values, demonstrates that one element of Christian exclusivity has been eroded. Moral renewal is not the exclusive preserve of religion and its institutions; the secular state can be an engine of ethical growth, informed by popular commitment to social justice. In abandoning the narrow conception of the Christian monopoly of morality, Tawney's thought has changed, belying the claim of essentialist commentators that the *Commonplace Book* stands as the best representative of his thought and the core of his subsequent work. We now turn to examine Tawney's first sustained expression of his political thought, *The Acquisitive Society*, where we find a rather more ambiguous picture.

3.5 *The Acquisitive Society* (1921)

In 1920, Tawney published an essay for the Fabian society, entitled *The Sickness of an Acquisitive Society*. The book, *The Acquisitive Society*, published the following year, is an expanded version of this essay, with a more thorough critique of liberalism and the inclusion of a discussion of the function of the Church in modern society (Tawney 1921: 17–22; 224–240). Commentators are correct in asserting its importance within the Tawney canon. Terrill (1973: 53) declares it to be 'one of the great books of the 1920s', while Reisman (1987: 91) claims that it reveals Tawney to be a man of 'prescience and perception' who 'raised questions which are in truth as much a challenge to our own times as to the, in so many ways, very different world of the 1920s'. The influence of the work within the Labour Party has been captured by Marquand (1999: 62), when he states that 'Tawney's doctrine was repeated, with varying degrees of eloquence and emphasis, from a thousand Labour platforms'. The supposed contemporary relevance of the piece has also been trumpeted by Duff (2004: 418), who argues that Tawney's concepts, embedded as they are in an industrial society, can be applied to the modern digital society, in that Tawney offers a 'normative as opposed to technocratic or historicist approach to the development of an information society'. However, Duff's catapulting of Tawney into cyberspace leads him to commit what Skinner (1969: 7–16) calls the 'mythology of doctrines' by criticizing Tawney's 'failure to theorise globalisation in any serious way' (Duff, 2004: 415).[1] Whatever its twenty-first century resonance, *The Acquisitive Society* is one of Tawney's most important works because it is the first detailed elaboration of his political theory, and an essential text for understanding the basis and character of his early political thought. Indeed, it is tempting to consider the work as effectively a summation of Tawney's ambivalent scholarship from 1914 to 1921, in that it is a creative synthesis of the abstract, Christian framework of the Diaries with the practical, secular emphasis of *The Conditions of Economic Liberty*. This synthesis is seen best in Tawney's treatment of the key concepts of Function, rights, property, capitalism, guild socialism, and religion.

3.5.1 Function

Function is the core concept of *The Acquisitive Society*, serving not only as the moral standard by which capitalism is held to account and found wanting, but also as the organizational ideal of the new order, and the foundation of other concepts such as property, rights and duties. Tawney's derivation of the term 'Function' is a matter of controversy. Wright (1987: 58–63) notes that although it was an idea that was prevalent within the guild socialist movement to which Tawney belonged, because his usage of the concept differs from other guild socialists, Tawney's historical study of medieval social relations is the more likely source, with its affinity to conventions of service, duty and obligation. Greenleaf (1983: 454) also mentions the medieval possibility, as well as the influence of John Ruskin, but concludes that the once fashionable guild socialist, Ramiro de Maezzu, is the most probable source. This last assertion is difficult

---

1   It is worth noting that Tawney himself drew attention to the illegitimacy of projecting issues upon political theorists that were only relevant to later times: 'The great individualists of the eighteenth century, Jefferson and Turgot and Condorcet and Adam Smith, shot their arrows against the abuses of their day, not ours. It is as absurd to criticise them as indifferent to the evils of a social order which they could not anticipate, as to appeal to their authority in defence of it' (Tawney, 1921: 19–20).

to accept because Greenleaf does not present any evidence to vali-
date it, but the influence of Ruskin should not be ignored, particularly as just before the publication of the Fabian essay that was
developed into *The Acquisitive Society*, Tawney produced an article
for the *Observer* devoted to Ruskin's ideas on industrial society
(Tawney, 1964b: 40–44). In this article, Tawney sketches many of
the ideas that subsequently appeared in *The Acquisitive Society*, with
particular reference to concepts such as social purpose and the
pre-eminence of the community that are intimately connected to
Ruskin's affection for pre-industrial society and his advocacy of
guilds.

Tawney defines Function in terms of 'social purpose':

> A Function may be defined as an activity which embodies and
> expresses the idea of social purpose... The essence of it is that
> the agent does not perform it merely for personal gain or to
> gratify himself, but recognises that he is responsible for its dis-
> charge to some higher authority. (Tawney, 1921: 9)

The act must be animated by a sense of moral duty, and this duty is
deontological rather than consequential. The primacy of motive or
intention over consequence ensures that any positive benefits acci-
dentally accrued cannot be admitted into the moral arena covered
by Tawney's conception of Function. Moreover, the act must reflect
individuals' conscious recognition of their obligation: subcon-
scious, habitual or accidental adherence to a social purpose is
incompatible with Tawney's belief in moral motivation. This is
underlined by the fact that Tawney often stresses the moral responsibility and, indeed, culpability of individuals (Tawney, 1921: 104;
111; 167; 191; 196): humans must ultimately be held accountable for
the contribution that their actions make to the public good. Tawney
was thus rejecting the shift of emphasis during the seventeenth century from common ends to private interests (Tawney, 1921: 12–24).
However, although Function is an uncompromising moral concept
that has human volition at its nucleus, perhaps contradictorily, it
also has an element of external determinism: individuals are 'instruments of a social purpose' (Tawney, 1921: 54).

The final point to notice about Function is Tawney's ambiguous
reference to 'some higher authority'. In his historical description of
the disappearance of Social Function, he associates the concept with

mankind's common relationship with God and the involvement of the Church within the social sphere, thereby endowing the concept with religious significance in the spirit of the Diaries, though the *Commonplace Book* does not provide a systematic elaboration of the idea of Function. However, Tawney sometimes depicts the higher authority not as a supernatural entity, but as the community at large, following in the spirit of *The Conditions of Economic Liberty*. This ambiguity raises the question of what happens if the community at large fails to acknowledge the concept of Function? In other words, what would happen if the democratic will of the people supported a programme that departed from the Functional theory that Tawney argues is central to the creation of a new society? Would Tawney justify the imposition of Social Function by the Church on behalf of the higher authority of God?

Having explored the meaning of Function, and noted its affinity with Tawney's pre-war position, we now turn to its practical application, beginning with Tawney's theory of rights.

3.5.2 Rights

In the analysis of the *Commonplace Book*, rights were subsumed under duties. Tawney there argued that the need to fulfil obligations is engrained in the human psyche and that individuals act in terms of the collective good founded on Christian norms. Abandoning the ideas on natural rights that he had enunciated in *The New Leviathan*, Tawney, in *The Acquisitive Society*, follows the Diaries in vigorously protesting against a rights-based society, in which the development of 'freedoms' associated with economic expansion marked the retreat of morality from the social sphere (Tawney, 1921: 10–18). Tawney here claims that the notion of absolute rights occupies a place of particular prominence in the developing acquisitive society:

> Henceforward they were thought to be absolute and indefeasible, and to stand by their own virtue. They were the ultimate political and social reality; and since they were the ultimate reality, they were not subordinate to other aspects of society, but other aspects of society were subordinate to them. (Tawney, 1921: 14)

Employing the idea we have previously termed English exception-alism, Tawney demonstrates how the transformation from defen-sive to active rights pioneered in France was altered when transplanted to Britain (Tawney, 1921: 16–18). Tawney argues that until the French Revolution, rights in Britain were defensive mech-anisms used to preserve individual liberty from the encroachments of the state. However, after the tumult across the channel, rights in Britain were transformed into positive claims that were the main principles of social organization; they became an assertive doctrine that made demands on government. Tawney claims that the abstract creed of the Rights of Man was inappropriate to the English national disposition because of its doctrinal and revolutionary basis; consequently it was narrowed from an all-embracing princi-ple to an expedient that facilitated the pursuit of commercial advantage. This reflected and reinforced the political philosophy expounded by Adam Smith, which suggested a natural affinity between the assertion of economic rights and the public good.

In *The Acquisitive Society*, Tawney deprecates any notion of rights as a basic attribute of human nature. He points out that natural rights are attractive to a capitalist society because they appeal to the powerful human instinct of acquisition (Tawney, 1921: 33), but he claims that they are one of the most prominent deformations that scar modern society. The maturation of modern rights theory is emblematic of the loss of social purpose, and the privileging of indi-vidual entitlements over the interests of the community (Tawney, 1921: 33; 96). The atomized society in which individuals are given absolute entitlement to pursue their economic interests has extin-guished the moral criteria that used to exist in pre-industrial soci-ety, and has resulted in a materialistic society relentlessly driven by accumulation. In other words, for Tawney, the contemporary ele-vation of rights above the communal needs of society is a signal of decline into a possessive individualism in which common ends are banished to the periphery. In line with the general tenor of the Dia-ries, Tawney deprecated the elevation of rights to 'absolute and indefeasible' entities that 'stand by their own virtue' and become the 'ultimate political and social reality' to which other aspects of society are subordinate (Tawney, 1921: 14). Although this invective is primarily aimed at what he would later term 'secondary liberties', which are entitlements that generally relate to economic activity, his argument here is unequivocally designed to show that every right is limited:

> All rights, in short are conditional and derivative because all power should be conditional and derivative. They are derived from the end or purpose of the society in which they exist. They are conditional on being used to the attainment of that end, not to thwart it. And this means in practice that, if society is to be healthy, men must regard themselves not as owners of rights, but as trustees for the discharge of functions and instruments of a social purpose. (Tawney, 1921: 54)

So Tawney's opposition to abstract rights is total. No rights can function independently of the social sphere, or occupy a privileged position relative to other values (Carter, 2003: 175). The inherent conditionality of rights is underlined when Tawney discusses the corrective to modern individualism:

> Society should be organised primarily for the performance of *duties*, not the maintenance of *rights*, and that the rights which it protects are those which are necessary to the discharge of social obligations. But duties, unlike rights, are relative to some end or purpose, for the sake of which they are imposed. The latter are a principle of division; they enable men to resist. The former are a principle of union; they lead men to co-operate. (Tawney, 1921: 96)

This statement rearticulates one of the important themes of the *Commonplace Book*—that rights need to be subsumed by duties to attain legitimacy. As Tawney states in *The Acquisitive Society*, individuals are 'instruments of a social purpose' (Tawney, 1921: 54). The notions of a sphere of liberty in which the individual is free of obligations, or a realm in which we can pursue inferior activities purely for the sake of enjoyment, are absent from Tawney's high-minded concept of liberty. As in the Diaries, in *The Acquisitive Society*, Tawney adopts an austere approach to rights, especially economic rights:

> No one has any business to expect to be paid 'what he is worth', for what he is worth is a matter between his own soul and God. What he has a right to demand, and what it concerns his fellow-men to see he gets, is enough to enable him to perform his

work... If a man has important work, and enough leisure and income to enable him to do it properly, he is in possession of as much happiness as is good for any of the children of Adam. (Tawney, 1921: 221)

In *The Acquisitive Society*, Tawney does recognize that consumption appetites are important, conceding that those who pursue a profession are 'influenced to some considerable, though uncertain, extent by economic incentive', although the extra efforts that may be expended in the pursuit of a profession should depend on more elevated values, such as social esteem and the traditions of service (Tawney, 1921: 193–194). But he reminds his readers that the proper needs of mankind entitle them to only sufficient material resources necessary to perform their social functions. In *The Acquisitive Society*, the argument against luxury items is not based only on moral disapproval, but also on practical grounds:

> Thus part of the goods which are annually produced, and which is called wealth, is, strictly speaking, waste, because it consists of articles which, though reckoned as a part of the income of the nation, either should not have been produced until other articles had already been produced in sufficient abundance, or should not have been produced at all. (Tawney, 1921: 40)

In line with the Diaries, Tawney deplores the utilitarian logic that governs acquisitive societies:

> If asked the end or criteria of social organisation, they would give the answer reminiscent of the formula the greatest happiness of the greatest number. But to say that the end of social institutions is happiness is to say that they have no common end at all. For happiness is individual, and to make happiness the object is to resolve society itself into the ambitions of numberless individuals, each directed towards the attainment of some personal purpose. (Tawney, 1921: 32)

Happiness is associated with atomistic tendencies, which detract from the collective duties and values we should all fulfil. Tawney's concept of rights is devoid of any discussion of happiness, and is not concerned to accommodate a principle of pleasure or delineate a sphere in which the individual is free from the demands of domestic and social duties. Indeed, rights in themselves are inherently divisive, because their assertion restricts the capacity of the community to function cohesively. This position must be viewed in the context of Tawney's acceptance of parliamentary democracy and his argument that the state itself, like the citizen, possesses no absolute rights, being bound by a commission of service (Tawney, 1921: 53). Of course, this does not mean that Tawney rejects any notion of rights: on the contrary, he strongly defends a notion of conditional rights, such as the conditional right to private property.

3.5.3 Property

In the *Commonplace Book*, Tawney's discussion of private property was limited, despite his conviction that its existence constitutes one of the main divisions in society. Implicit in the Diaries is the idea that the concentrated ownership of property is the major source of class power, leaving the dispossessed dependent on the bourgeoisie for the maintenance of their existence, but Tawney did not begin to address the question from a more practical angle until the publication of *The Conditions of Economic Liberty*, where he stated that private ownership would not necessarily be prohibited in the new society (Tawney, 1964b: 111). *The Acquisitive Society* enlarges on these themes, presenting a historical theory of property that rejects the extremism of both opponents and advocates of private property.

Tawney identifies two diametrically opposed theories of property. There is the *socialistic* view that private property is inherently wrong, serving as the foundation stone of inequality and in need of communal appropriation; and there is the *conservative* standpoint which regards the possession of property as an inviolable right, with owners free to dispose of their holdings as they see fit (Tawney, 1921: 55–57). Both positions — uncompromising abolitionism, and unqualified apologism — are dismissed by Tawney:

> The idea of some socialists that private property in land or capital is necessarily mischievous is a piece of scholastic pedantry as absurd as that of those Conservatives who would invest all property with some kind of mysterious sanctity. (Tawney, 1921: 99)

Applying his concept of Function, Tawney argues that modes of property ownership are legitimate to the extent that they make an active contribution to the social purpose, and to the extent that those in a position of ownership are motivated by, and act in accordance with, their social duties. 'Active' is the operative word, because explicit in Tawney's argument is that owners of property must be fully engaged in the productive process; the position of the passive shareholder is unacceptable. In Tawney's view, the main division of capitalism is not between owners and non-owners of property, but between active and passive owners of property, because the passive beneficiaries live off the constructive efforts of the active (Tawney, 1921: 90). The essential passivity of capital, in that it is useless without the intervention of human labour, suggests Marx's labour theory of value. But Tawney rejects Marx's identification of the major cleavage in society between the bourgeoisie and proletariat, and instead sees the main class antagonism between those who use their creative powers, and those who reap rewards without expending any intellectual or physical effort.

Tawney's ideal conception of property is exemplified in pre-industrial society — particularly in medieval property relations (Tawney, 1921: 63–64). He lays down three conditions for an acceptable property regime. The first condition is a wide dispersal of productive property, to ensure that most citizens are afforded a degree of security and not dependent on the whims of a single individual or company (though whether medieval property relations met this condition is unclear). Second, the property that people own has to be the main source of their livelihood, ensuring that their creative powers are fruitfully employed, because the relationship between property and the cultivation of human capacity is of fundamental importance to Tawney. He denounces the situation which found:

> mankind... shovelled like raw material into an economic mill,
> to be pounded and ground and kneaded into the malleable
> human pulp out of which national prosperity and power, all the
> kingdoms of the world and the glory of them are supposed to
> be manufactured. (Tawney, 1921: 97–98)

Echoes of the pre-war Tawney are evident in his assertion that passive owners pervert the values of society because the creative talents of the labourer and scientist are subordinated to the needs of passive accumulation. Third, property has to be embedded in a nexus of legal strictures that impose obligations on the owners to produce to meet the needs of the community rather than for individual profit.

On the question of how to enforce these conditions, Tawney reveals elements of Fabianism (Tawney, 1921: 93–95; 102–103). He argues that private enterprise is unable to reform itself because it is intrinsically inefficient: given the priority it accords to the passive shareholder, indolence and acquisitiveness are defining characteristics of the system. This entails a dearth of innovation and the stagnation of society, because parasitic capitalists prefer to procure short-term profits than to invest in more efficient productive techniques. In passages reminiscent of the arguments of Sydney Webb, Tawney writes of the inevitable expansion of the state into the economic sphere to eliminate waste, protect the consumer, and improve economic performance (Tawney, 1921: 152).

However, Tawney insists that nationalization should not be elevated into a principled objective, nor should it be seen as the only means of reforming capitalist relations. The state appropriation of economic units is only a means of attaining social ends, not an end in itself. Public ownership should not be considered as an article of faith; rather it is a practical policy that may be expedient in certain circumstances. This refusal to privilege one form of ownership over another is further demonstrated when Tawney cites a range of socially acceptable modes of economic organization, including co-operative management, guild systems, and local authority appropriation. Significantly, he proposes a transitional stage, in which private owners are denied any control of economic enterprises, and are paid a fixed rate of interest on their investment to ensure that their extraction of monies in severely limited (Tawney, 1921: 123–124). While Tawney does not describe such an arrangement as desirable, and it would only be transitory, it demonstrates the flexibility of his theory of property, and reflects a conception of the economy as an arena of experimentation with different forms of ownership co-existing and being maintained, providing that they fulfil Functional objectives.

3.5.4 Capitalism

Several of Tawney's ideas on capitalism have already been touched on in previous sections. In this section, we will focus on the account he gives in *The Acquisitive Society* of the breakdown of the capitalist system. Before the publication of *The Acquisitive Society*, Tawney paid little attention to the practical dynamics of creating and sustaining a progressive alternative to capitalism. The Diaries, while displaying a vehement distaste for the existing order, omitted to identify a means of change, beyond the simplistic notion that the level of pre-war dissatisfaction was indicative of a movement for reform inspired by the oratory of the street corner preacher. In *The Conditions of Economic Liberty*, Tawney suggested that the crystallizing experience of conflict exposed the ideological fallacies and structural frailties of capitalism, and stimulated a renewed optimism in the capacity of the populace to seek change. *The Acquisitive Society* builds on this suggestion, and presents a discourse of collapse, with a profound sense that the cataclysm of war and the succeeding economic tumult has generated an intellectual and structural transformation, heralding the disintegration of the capitalist system. This intellectual transformation has not, however, come easily to the phlegmatic English temperament:

> The blinkers worn by Englishmen enable them to trot all the more steadily along the beaten road, without being disturbed by the curiosity as to their destination... There are times which are not ordinary, and in such times it is not enough to follow the road... it must have a clear apprehension both of the deficiency of what is, and the character of what ought to be. And to obtain this apprehension it must appeal to some standard more stable than the momentary exigencies of its commerce or industry or social life, and judge them by it. It must, in short, have recourse to Principles. (Tawney, 1921: 1–3)

English sceptical empiricism, which prefers practical activity to intellectual scrutiny of the fundamental basis of society, is an impediment in a country in need of direction. The traditional English way of avoiding grand historic leaps, and extolling the traditions that serve as the nation's reference point when upheaval threatens, is redundant in a society pulverized by war and characterized by a failing philosophy. The only way to avoid economic and social disaster is to persuade the English temperament to embrace principles, and according to Tawney, this depends on popular acknowledgment of the seriousness of the threats facing the country. He sees his role as publicizing those threats.

The immediate context in which Tawney wrote revealed a glaring contradiction between the inflated rhetoric of Prime Minister David Lloyd George, with his desire to create a country fit for heroes to live in, and the stuttering programme of social renewal accompanied by recession. These economic tribulations culminated in the infamous Geddes Axe, with the government introducing severe public expenditure cuts. In this picture of stagnation and broken promises, Tawney detected the signs of systemic destruction:

> The first symptom of its collapse is what the first symptom of economic collapses has usually been in the past — the failure of customary stimuli to evoke their customary response in human effort. (Tawney, 1921: 173)

The vulnerability of the system is evident because of the ineffectual nature of the disciplines traditionally used to cement the employer/employee relationship (Tawney, 1921: 173–178). The main driving force of capitalism, the labour power of individuals, is no longer functioning in a manner conducive to the preservation of the system. The historical operation of the economy depended on the compliance of the workers; an objective obtained by the twin threats of hunger and fear. The workers' dependence on a living wage for basic subsistence ensured that they had an interest in maintaining the status quo. The threat of arbitrary dismissal acted as an effective constraint on forms of behaviour that threatened upheaval. So Tawney, while stressing the barbaric nature of this regime, conceded that it generated a degree of efficiency. However, this supportive structure is beginning to implode for three reasons. First, the efficiency gains that undermined criticism of the system are no longer apparent. Second, post-war attitudinal change has eroded the willingness of the populace to tolerate industrial inhumanity: employers are now faced by increasingly truculent workers. Third, legislative change has provided a welfare safety net for sacked workers, in the form of the nascent welfare state, with the Unemployment Insurance Act. While Tawney regarded the level of this welfare provision as woefully inadequate, he saw it as a part of

a rolling programme of amelioration, which would eventually lead
to a comprehensive system of support. The effect of these three factors is a radical shift in economic power from capitalist to worker:

> It is a tyrant who must intrigue and cajole where formerly he
> commanded, a gaoler who, if not yet deprived of the whip, dare
> only to administer moderate chastisement, and who, though he
> still protests that he alone can keep the treadmill moving and
> get the corn ground, is compelled to surrender so much author-
> ity as to make it questionable whether he is worth his keep.
> (Tawney, 1921: 175)

However, for Tawney, unlike other democratic socialists, this process does not herald the permanent amelioration of the capitalist
system. For other socialists, efforts to forge a historic class compromise with the foundation of the welfare state are seen as an attempt
to confound Marxism by blunting the worst excesses of capitalism.
But Tawney's theory of collapse rejects this argument: in his view,
the workers have not been bought off or integrated into the system
by reformist measures; on the contrary, the prospect of a guaran-
teed social minimum has emboldened them to demand more radical change. While Tawney commended social reforms such as the
Minimum Rates Acts and the National Insurance Scheme, his clear
perception is that reform within the system is not sufficient to alle-
viate the profound problems of industrial society. Direct experience
of the operation of the factory system with its waste and inefficiency has persuaded the worker to see 'the claim of the capitalist to
be the self-appointed guardian of public interests as a piece of sanc-
timonious hypocrisy' (Tawney, 1921: 178). The worker's attitude,
galvanized by education and experience, accompanied by the
structural changes already outlined, is penetrating the mythology
of capitalist superiority. This psychological shift is not a transitory
or temporary reaction to cyclical readjustment; rather it is a permanent fixture that exposes the mortality of the system:

> It is as impossible to restore them, to revive by mere exhortation
> the complex of hopes and fears and ignorance and patient cre-
> dulity and passive acquiescence, which together made men,
> fifty years ago, plastic instruments in the hands of industrial-
> ism, as to restore innocence to any others of those who have
> eaten at the tree of knowledge. (Tawney, 1921: 182)

Another feature of Tawney's theory of the imminent demise of capitalism differentiates his analysis from that of revolutionary socialists—the role of the managerial class. Unlike the socialist class
warriors, Tawney does not see managers as the enemy (Tawney,
1921: 203–204), but rather as ultimately allied to their fellow
wage-earners. Managers are themselves alienated from the system
they administer because they are denied control of economic enterprises and do not share in the profits they help to generate. Mired in
a system of favouritism and nepotism in which they witness the
owners promoting their sons on the basis of family ties rather than
competence, they are placed in an invidious position:

> Regarded by the workmen as the hangers-on of the masters,
> and by their employers as one section amongst the 'hands', they
> have the odium of capitalism without its power or profits.
> (Tawney, 1921: 204)

Tawney hints that given the conditions that the managerial class
have to endure, it is probable that, just like the working class, they
will realize that the root of their discontent is the capitalist system,
and they will accept the necessity of its replacement by a Functional
Society. This wide coalition of groupings shows that the clamour
for change comes not from a strict class division, with different
classes' reactions determined by the impact of the system on their
relative economic positions. Rather it is the moral revulsion felt by
the broad mass of humanity subjected to a system which restricts its
creative input; denies it the degree of power proportionate to its
active contribution; and regards it as a mere instrument of production. So for Tawney, the source of resistance rests not so much with
narrow class interests as with the moral instincts of humanity.

   This indicates that Tawney's theory of change is based on idealism rather than historical materialism—on the power of ideas
rather than the power of economic forces. He rejects the Marxian
notion of society inevitability moving towards socialism, with each
economic stage establishing the pre-requisites for the following
epoch. Tawney's discourse of collapse is derived from an appraisal
of existing tendencies within contemporary Britain, not an abstract,
teleological ideology of historical development. His advocacy of
change is fundamentally moral, so a theory of inevitability cannot
be accommodated in his thought because the doctrine of moral per-

suasion is premised on a conception of freedom. The action of the people in overthrowing the capitalist system would not constitute a moral act if it were merely a mechanical response of impersonal forces. The choice needs to be an expression of human volition rather than an automatic reaction to external stimuli. At this stage in his work, Tawney's denial of historical laws is implicit in his discussion of capitalist breakdown; in later years he would mount a full-scale attack on speculative philosophies of history as inherently totalitarian.

However, although human choice rather than historical determinism pulls the lever, Tawney describes that choice in terms of service to God, and in circumstances where the alternative to choosing socialism is war and the end of civilization:

> If the conditions which produce that unnatural tension are to be removed, it can only be effected by the growth of a habit of mind which will approach questions of economic organisation from the standpoint of the purpose which exists to serve, and which will apply to it something of the spirit expressed by Bacon when he said that the work of men ought to be carried on 'for the glory of God and the relief of men's estate.' Sentimental idealism? But consider the alternative. The alternative is war; and continuous war must, sooner or later, mean something like the destruction of civilisation. (Tawney, 1921: 223–224)

So while it is true that for Tawney, socialism was not the inevitable result of historical laws, it is also true that choosing socialism was not an act of completely free choice — there is a heavily-loaded moral imperative to opt into the Functional Society.

3.5.5 Guild socialism

In considering what form socialism would take in a post-capitalist Functional Society, Tawney was drawn to the ideas of guild socialism. Some commentators play down the importance of guild socialism in his thinking. For example, Terrill (1973: 142–143; 157) argues that Tawney has been over-identified with the movement, and that he was not really a guild socialist because of his reservations about the anti-democratic and sectional basis of the movement. It is true that Tawney himself stated that he was an unorthodox guild socialist, and it is also true that his membership of the guild organization is not conclusive evidence of allegiance, because he was also a member of the Fabian Society (a sworn enemy of guild socialism) from 1906 onwards, despite dissenting from many of its key ideas. However, there is a strong conceptual basis of a link between Tawney's socialism and guild ideas.

Tawney and the guild socialists shared some doctrines in common. For instance, the guild movement was based on an admiration of medieval society, where the independent artisan was able to exercise his skills in producing articles necessary to the functioning of the community. It is precisely these values of independence, communal service and self-expression that proved so appealing to socialists who were frustrated by Fabian collectivism. It has already been established that Tawney lamented the passing of the organizational ideals of pre-industrial society, and celebrated the benign poverty, social ethics and spiritual peace that supposedly characterized the Elizabethan era. Both Tawney and guild socialists like Pentry advanced a morally substantive conception of man which was inimical to the cold technocratic strategies proposed by the collectivists. This was succinctly expressed in a striking image in the *Commonplace Book*, when Tawney declared that Fabians 'tidy the room, but they open no windows in the soul' (Tawney, 1972: 51). The Fabian obsession with finding more efficient ways of organizing industry demonstrated the same preoccupation with productivity, but neglect of the human spirit, that characterized capitalism.

The practical organizational principles that Tawney advocates in *The Acquisitive Society* also reflect the ideas of guild socialism. He believed that the liberation of industry depended on its reorganization into professions, and he conceived of a profession as a group of workers who perform a function in accordance with rules to ensure that its members are better protected and the public receive a better standard of service (Tawney, 1921: 106). These professions, although conceived as organizational units with a range of powers to conduct their own affairs, are subordinate to the social purposes embodied in the will of the community.

However, two criticisms can be levelled at Tawney's advocacy of guild socialism. First, Tawney does not explain how the will of the community is to be identified under such a system of economic and social organization, let alone how that will is to be enforced. In short, he has not solved the problem of guild socialism's democratic deficit. Tawney holds an optimistic view that the self-regulating guilds will serve common ends rather than pursue their own self-interests, and that parliament would be the ultimate impediment to the guilds' power if they acted outside the Functional framework. But he does not spell out the mechanisms whereby this parliamentary control will be exercised, and as a consequence, he does not address the key criticism of guild socialism, acknowledged even by some early advocates like Bertrand Russell, that the system could empower worker's organizations at the expense of democracy. Moreover, Tawney does not discuss how far the franchise should be extended; the role of parties in society; or the way they should function in parliament. It seems that, while his intention to subordinate the guilds to the community is transparently sincere in principle, the practical means to secure this have not been thought out.

The second criticism is that Tawney fails to remove another weakness of the guild system — that it allows the sectional interest of the producers to dominate, and as a result, the interests of the consumer are neglected. It was this concern that troubled collectivist socialists and also liberals who were otherwise sympathetic to guild ideas (Freeden, 1986: 69–71). While the preference for internal regulation, rather than state supervision, is a natural offshoot of guild socialism's advocacy of decentralized workers' institutions and its rejection of the over-active state, Tawney's faith in producer power does raise questions about the capacity of consumers to protect themselves from coercive producer power. It is true that he tries to address this consumer deficit by including a reference to effective service to the public within his definition of a profession, and that he affirms that public control and criticism of guilds is essential (Tawney, 1921: 106; 187). However, he is not clear about how this control will be exercised, and this creates doubts about the strength of his consumer safeguards. These uncertainties are compounded by Tawney's warning that scrutiny should not be excessively detailed, and that once fair standards have been established, the professions should operate on the basis of self-regulation (Tawney, 1921: 187).

One possible solution to these two problems is categorically rejected by Tawney — the collectivist socialist solution of nationalization. In common with other guild socialists, Tawney did not see any axiomatic relationship between public ownership and the self-development of the workers or the protection of consumers. While he praised the commitment of public servants in administering nationalized industries, he stressed that they 'were not of the craft' and could 'hardly have feel of it in their figures' (Tawney, 1921: 187). This demonstrates Tawney's belief that the members of a profession, who are imbued with the traditions of their craft and possess a direct relationship with the act of production, are best qualified to run their industries, and to satisfy their customers. So Tawney's answer to these criticisms amount to an article of faith: underlying his faith in guild socialism was his assumption that it would generate a new economic mentality, which in turn would remove both the democratic and consumer deficits. He believed that the system would foster a transformed economic psychology, which would ensure harmonious relations and greater efficiency (Tawney, 1921: 184–191). The capitalist system's reliance on coercion to reproduce itself generated profound hostility amongst the workforce, who viewed their economic function purely in terms of survival, impeding the creation of a professional spirit. The fact that greater efforts by the workers delivered increased dividends for the shareholders, gave the workers little incentive to improve performance. It was only through the creation of professional sentiments that efficiency could be attained, sentiments that depended on such factors as self-esteem, the force of public opinion, and the laudable traditions of the profession:

> In all cases where difficult and disagreeable work is done, the force which elicits it is normally not merely money, but the public opinion and the tradition of the little society in which the individual moves, and in the esteem of which he finds that which men value in success. (Tawney, 1921: 186)

Tawney's presumption, which was a key feature of his early political thought, that humans are motivated by more edifying incentives than monetary gain, applied to a guild system which was both a cause and effect of the new economic psychology (Tawney, 1921: 191–201). Tawney sees guild socialism as sustained by a vigorous system of vocational education that not only imparts the technical aspects of a craft, but cultivates the values conducive to an enlightened, meritocratic, and moral society:

> It would emphasize that there are certain things – like advertising, or accepting secret commissions, or taking advantage of client's ignorance, or rigging the market, or other analogous practices of the present commercial world – which 'the services can't do'. It would cultivate the *esprit de corps* which is natural to young men, and would make them feel that to snatch special advantages for oneself, like any other common business man is... an odious offence against good manners. (Tawney, 1921: 196)

However, despite Tawney's conviction that the capitalist system was entering its final stages, and that the war had generated a shift in attitudes, it is clear that the creation of this new society will require a long period of transition. The complete break with the habits developed under capitalism, not to mention the organizational revolution proposed, cannot be achieved without considerable effort and perseverance.

So Tawney had moved his theory away from the morally certain, but practically bereft, *Commonplace Book*, to one in which he was actively proposing new political and economic institutions which demonstrate an affinity with guild socialism. Guild socialism served as the catalyst that allowed Tawney to transform the Christian exhortations of the Diaries into a more concrete programme designed for practical implementation that recognized the capacity of the secular state to assist in the creation of an edifying society. Had Tawney allowed the original pamphlet (*The Sickness of an Acquisitive Society*) to pass into publication, the perception that he had become a largely secular thinker would be irresistible. If readers of the pamphlet had any knowledge of the Diaries, they would have noted that Tawney had moved from assigning a significant role to the Church in the new society, to one in which secular political and economic institutions founded to address contemporary problem held sway – a process of change discernible in his mid-war essays. However, Tawney added a final chapter to *The Acquisitive Society* which throws this secularized interpretation into confusion.

3.5.6 Religion

In the final chapter of *The Acquisitive Society*, Tawney provides a religious foundation for his otherwise almost entirely secular case for socialism. The new co-operative economic spirit of the post-capitalist society, which is essential to the pursuit and attainment of common ends, is here given a Christian root:

> Such a political philosophy implies that society is not an economic mechanism, but a community of wills which are often discordant, but which are capable of being inspired by a devotion to common ends. It is, therefore, a religious one, and, if it is true, the proper bodies to propagate it are the Christian Churches. (Tawney, 1921: 227)

This belated re-introduction of the Church as the vehicle of the ethical consensus that is a pre-requisite for fundamental change, while not a return to the Christian exclusivity of the *Commonplace Book*, does, in the absence of any discussion of the role of political parties, accord major significance to the Church as a political player. In the analysis of the Diaries, it was unclear how the Church could stimulate ethical rejuvenation without embroiling itself in the moral morass of political affairs, but here Tawney makes it clear that the Church needs to intervene in the social sphere, although, as in the Diaries, the precise form that this intervention will take remains opaque. In this final chapter of *The Acquisitive Society*, he rehearses the historical abjuration of the post-medieval Church, when it surrendered responsibility for enforcing a body of ethics to the political and economic realm. As a result, Christian ethics degenerated from an active social doctrine to a personal moral code, largely unconcerned with the economic practices that it would once have condemned as sinful. In Tawney's words, 'they made religion the ornament of leisure, instead of the banner of a Crusade' (Tawney, 1921: 233). While he is careful not to glorify the operation of the preceding medieval Church, the thrust of Tawney's narrative indicates that the Church needs to re-conjure up the spirit of that period and re-engage with social reality, to wage war against capitalism.

So the concluding chapter of the book transforms our perception of the preceding chapters. In Tawney's discussion of rights and duties in the main body of the work, with the need for rights to be conditional and derivative, it is clear that Tawney is referring to the community as the superior body. But, in the final chapter, he reverts to the formulations of the *Commonplace Book* to suggest that our shared relationship with God is the basis for our equal status, and underlines the notion that rights are a commission of service (Tawney, 1921: 234).

The robustness of Tawney's religious belief is further demonstrated when he discusses the internal discipline and religious mission of the Church (Tawney, 1921: 237–239). Christians must rigidly follow Christian teachings in the conduct of their social affairs, and pagans must be converted by the Church to Christianity. So not only does Tawney accord the Church the main role in securing the essential moral consensus necessary for renewal, but he also suggests it has the capacity to convert. While he deprecates the religious abuse that has been employed against the non-believer — the slaughtered heretic should not be the catalyst for the acceptance of Christianity — Tawney is adamant that the purity of the religious doctrine is not to be blemished by diluting its precepts to appeal to the agnostic or atheist. Indeed, it is precisely its doctrinal rigidity that is its source of strength:

> It will appeal to mankind, not because its standards are identical with those of the world, but because they are profoundly different. It will win its converts, not because membership involves no change in their manner of life, but because it involves a change so complete as to be ineffaceable. It will expect its adherents to face economic ruin for the sake of their principles. (Tawney, 1921: 239)

So Tawney does not propose a religious/secular *rapprochement* or accommodation; the integrity of the Christian doctrine with its gospel-inspired concept of right and wrong must be preserved — though, as in the Diaries, he does not explain how the Church will carry out its mission role in the political sphere.

3.6 Conclusion

This chapter has traced the evolution of Tawney's thoughts from the *Commonplace Book* to the first of his three major books[2] on political theory, *The Acquisitive Society*. We have shown that the six works Tawney published during this period—a lecture, four essays and a book—reveal a gradual change from a religious-based to a secular-based political theory, though *The Acquisitive Society* unexpectedly concludes with a religious coping to an otherwise predominantly secular analysis. In the first work, an inaugural lecture, Tawney rejects the social Darwinist view that poverty is due to the inherent inferiority of the poor rather than to economic conditions. The first two essays, *The Attack* and *Some Reflections of a Soldier*, which are the direct result of Tawney's military service during the First World War, while reinforcing the doctrine of original sin presented in the Diaries, move away from the Diaries' emphasis on class conflict to the clash between civilians and returning soldiers. The remaining two essays, *National College of All Souls* and *The Conditions of Economic Liberty*, mark a shift from the abstract and pessimistic tone of the first two essays to a practical and constructive mode, exemplified, for example, in Tawney's advocacy of universal education, to be achieved through a positive role played by the state. The chasm between civilian and soldier had been bridged by a collective acceptance of the moral basis of such reform. In the book— *The Acquisitive Society*—many of these themes (especially those put forward in *The Conditions of Economic Liberty*) are reinforced and absorbed into a framework of 'Function', wherein social purpose rather than private profit motivates the workforce and conditions the principles of rights and property. Here Tawney presents an idealist explanation of the breakdown of materialistic capitalism and its replacement by an austere form of guild socialism. Most of this analysis draws on secular argumentation, until, in the final chapter of the book, Tawney states that underpinning this transformation is a moral revolution which is rooted in Christian values. As Dell (2000: 15–16) rightly comments: 'His text frequently lapses into the language of the pulpit, with the menacing content of

---

2   The other two major books are *Religion and the Rise of Capitalism* (1926) and *Equality* (1931).

hell as well as the promise of heaven'. Here Tawney appears to turn back towards the *Commonplace Book*, at least in one important respect, locating the key to social reform in Christian doctrine and attributing to the Church an active role in converting secular minds to a spiritual understanding of the basis of that reform. However, Stefan Collini (1998), in his critical assessment of *The Acquisitive Society*, has a persuasive interpretation of this apparent shift. Echoing Beatrice Webb's puzzlement over Tawney's Christian beliefs, who noted Tawney's reluctance to discuss his faith; his dislike of theological pontificating; and the relative absence of religious references in his work, Collini states that:

> Structurally (and, one cannot help suspecting, psychologically), the overriding importance of Christianity for Tawney at this point is simply that it out-trumps economic criteria. It is the organised assertion of an alternative standard of values that he seeks, values to which economic reasoning would be subordinate, and in the light of which proximate goals and purposes could be identified in moral, non-economic terms. (Collini, 1998: 95)

This sense that Tawney's Christianity may not have been the driving force of his work, but, at least in 1921, a convenient framework to criticize capitalism, is not purely derived from the content of *The Acquisitive Society*, but also from biographical material. Collini (1998: 95; 96) asserts that the 'biographical evidence leaves the nature of Tawney's own religious beliefs opaque', suggesting that 'it is hard not to feel that he was drawn to social Christianity because it provided a language with which to censure the unfettered pursuit of material gain; one doesn't get the sense that it was his belief in Christian principles that led him to become such a severe critic of economic self-interest'.

Moreover, this belated re-assertion of the centrality of religion in bringing about the socialist dawn is short-lived, as we shall see in the next chapter. During the next period (1922–1925), Tawney's practical involvement in the realm of politics deepens as his writings on the education system contribute to Labour Party policy. His academic career takes him to Yale, where his lectures on the British Labour Movement form the basis of a much neglected book, which throws considerable light on the development of his political theory. Tawney was beginning to move into areas which would entail even greater engagement with the practical and secular world of politics.

Chapter Four

Learning to Labour (1922–1925)

Education: The Socialist Policy (1924)
The British Labour Movement (1925)

4.1 Introduction

Tawney's involvement with political organizations was extensive, in that at various times, and often simultaneously, he held membership of the Independent Labour Party, the Fabian Society, the Guild Socialist Movement and the Labour Party. While all being located on the left flank of the British political world, maintaining concurrent membership did raise potential questions for Tawney, as was demonstrated in the previous chapter, with the profound gulf between what is often conceived as the technocratic monism of Fabianism and the autonomous decentralization advocated by the guild socialists, though such questions did not seem to trouble, or even register with, Tawney. His links with the Labour Party were the most deep-rooted and constant, and in the period 1921–1925 these links were forged by an increasing practical and intellectual engagement. On the practical side, Tawney was persuaded primarily by Sidney Webb to play an active role in formulating the education policy of the Labour Party. Webb had witnessed Tawney's performance on the Sankey Commission, which was established by Lloyd George to examine the future of the coal industry, and was impressed by his forensic questioning and the vigorous manner in which he asserted the interests of the trade unions. Tawney, confirming Webb's expectations, applied the same rigour to his analysis of public education, and he was instrumental in drafting Labour's policy published in 1922 under the title, *Secondary Education for All* (see Tawney, 1988).

   In this chapter, we focus, first, on Tawney's 1924 pamphlet, *Education: The Socialist Policy*, which addresses the democratic conundrum at the heart of Tawney's politics, and begins to expand on his seminal concept of equality. Second, we discuss Tawney's 1925 book (see Tawney, 1968), *The British Labour Movement*. Based on lectures delivered at Yale University, this book is relegated to the margins by most commentators, who seldom refer to it. However, when judged from the perspective of historical chronology, the book is highly significant because it represents Tawney's first thorough analysis of the function of political parties. In it, the Church-centric approach outlined in both the Diaries and final chapter of *The Acquisitive Society*, with the crusade of conversion necessary to the creation of the good society, is tempered by Tawney's acceptance that the Labour Party is an indispensable vehicle for the humane reform of the country.

4.2 *Education: The Socialist Policy* (1924)

Before Tawney contributed to Labour Party policy, it is clear that he viewed education as a vital part of any civilized society. His enthusiasm for, and involvement with, the WEA demonstrates his belief that education should be a universal entitlement and not rationed on the basis of wealth. Accessibility to the tools of learning was fundamental to crafting a human personality that could contribute to a person's surroundings. In the Diaries, where Tawney's Christian faith was pivotal, he imbued education with a sacramental significance that condemned its provision for monetary gain. After the war, Tawney regarded the extension of education as a legitimate call on the national debt; the obligation that was owed to classes who had ensured the survival of the British way of life. Even in *The*

Acquisitive Society, where his preoccupation with industrial organization eclipsed most other concerns, Tawney found space to highlight the importance of vocational education in transmitting the norms, both practical and moral, of a profession. From these works, it is clear that Tawney did not view education in isolation; rather he placed it in the context of other institutions, demonstrating how it impacted on the wider social environment. His pamphlet, *Education: The Socialist Policy*, enlarges on these themes and provides a more detailed account of the need for universal provision. We focus on two areas central to understanding Tawney's political stance: first, the contribution that individuality, nurtured by education, makes to a vibrant democracy; and second, how educational reform fits into the agenda for equality.

4.2.1 Individuality and democracy

Although Tawney's socialism accepts the liberal inheritance of constitutionalism and representative institutions, the precise nature of his commitment to democracy is uncertain. In his early writings, Tawney's adherence to the absolute truth of the Christian doctrine; his conviction that some fundamental political truths can be extracted from the religious firmament; and the lack of any discussion of the organs of political change, raise a number of questions about his attitude to democracy. However, *Education: The Socialist Policy* goes some way to reducing Tawney's incipient, if unintentional, authoritarianism by linking education to the development of an effective democracy:

> What is evident to-day, if one compares the practical operation of democracy with the anticipations formed by the school of Bentham and Mill, is that it is precisely in the weakness of the means by which men are prepared to form an intelligent opinion, in the liability of the individual to be overwhelmed by mass suggestions which he has not learned to criticise, in his reluctance to undertake on his own account, the painful process of analysis, and in the ease with which, as a consequence, he succumbs to the great modern art of organising delusion, that a capital weakness of our society consists. (Tawney, 1924: 4)

The purpose of this pamphlet is to show that education is pivotal to the creation of a critical mentality capable of discriminating between fact and fiction. Because the historical evolution of the education system has been dictated by the class structure, a large number of the population have been impeded in developing their mental faculties. Indeed, encouragement to engage in the difficult task of intellectual exploration has been deliberately withheld in order to produce a docility that suits the purposes of a plutocratic society. When Tawney speaks of 'the great modern art of organised delusion' he is referring to the propaganda imparted by politicians and the press, and this was forcefully conveyed in his thoughts about the ideological exploitation of the Great War. Equally, Tawney was concerned about the emerging advertising industry, which he berated as a form of quackery. This emphasis on resisting the superficially persuasive utterances of charlatans suggests that Tawney wants to develop a discerning and sophisticated electorate, able to make intelligent decisions. However, to propose the need for a sophisticated electorate does not in itself mean that Tawney has abandoned the moral monism expressed in the Diaries. He may still hold an absolutist conception of the right way sanctioned by Christian norms, and believe that the extension of knowledge will lead to the populace moving toward those norms. However, as Tawney's argument develops, his view of education is less prescriptive than this: indeed, at some points, he seems to regard education as an end in itself — a form of individual self-development:

> The first question to be asked in planning schools and curricula is not 'what does society think children ought to be?' but 'under what conditions do children develop most harmoniously and completely?' For the achievements of education are to be measured primarily by its success in assisting growth, not in imposing discipline or imparting information; and the problem is not to prepare children to fit into the moulds, or to acquire the formulae, thought desirable by the existing generation of adults, but to enable them, when they are children, to be healthy children, in order that when they are men they may define their own attitude to the world for themselves. (Tawney, 1924: 5)

The unfolding and development of the inherent talents of each child in a school system tailored to the distinctive needs of the individual and guided by an ethos of self-development is of value in its own right. For Tawney, the capacity to exercise independent judgment is an important human faculty, so education should be designed not to inculcate knowledge, but to nurture the spirit of individuality. Tawney believes that schools should be 'a centre radiating vitality amongst all children of the country' (Tawney, 1924: 12). He describes the teacher as a facilitator, rejecting the 'chalk and talk' conception whereby children unquestionably accept the wisdom imparted by their superior instructor:

> The attitude of stupefied awe, as of a sparrow before an accomplished, if capricious, serpent, which was not unknown nor (if reports may be trusted) wholly unvalued in the generation after 1870, has more and more been yielding to one in which the child is encouraged to turn to the teacher as a guide and friend. (Tawney, 1924: 20)

Nevertheless, by fostering a spirit of individuality in children, education would perform the valuable function of enhancing society's capacity to solve its common problems:

> Our problem to-day is… to enlist the active and critical intelligence of the rank and file in the solution of our common problems; it is to encourage willingness in the plain man to leave the rut and assume responsibility. (Tawney, 1924: 22)

Universal education would enable ordinary people to take the initiative by contributing to decision-making in political and in industrial life, thereby reducing the current democratic deficit in both spheres. This activist conception, while cohering with Tawney's conception of industrial democracy, departs from his discussion of rights and duties contained in the *Commonplace Book*, where rights did not have an independent existence from duties; rights were seen as desirable to the extent that they contributed to fulfilment of domestic and social obligations. By contrast, in *Education: The Socialist Policy*, the right to education appears to be primarily for the fulfilment of the individual, and secondarily for the social good. In other words, the right to education has taken on some of the features of a natural right, as enunciated by Tawney in *The New Leviathan*.

4.2.2 Equality

Equality is the concept that is most closely identified with Tawney, and it is in his analysis of education that it first emerges in a practical form. In *Education: The Socialist Policy*, Tawney's advocacy of equality is expressed in two principles: first, equal access to a decent education to all who can benefit; and second, entitlement to equal consideration of individual educational needs.

EQUALITY OF ACCESS TO EDUCATION

Tawney's argument for equal access to education is an attack on the contemporary education system which mirrored the deformations of the class structure, with the schooling of different groups formed by preconceived ideas about their future role in society (Tawney, 1924: 15; 16; 30). There was private education for the upper class; secondary education for the middle class; and elementary education for the working class. Class philosophy maintained that it is futile to educate those destined for the factory beyond a certain level, and several practical impediments prevented the working class accessing secondary schools, including a lack of places and the levying of fees. Although scholarships did exist, their effect was severely limited. Tawney presents a barrage of statistics throughout the work to show that through under-funding, lack of accommodation, and too few suitably qualified teachers, 85% of the population received no education beyond the age of 14 (Tawney, 1924: 26). Moreover, the elementary education that the working class did receive was woefully inadequate, with pupils being taught the basic rudiments by tutors without the requisite expertise, in crammed, dilapidated class rooms often accommodating 50 children. This litany of deprivation is an expression of a society geared to acquisitiveness, in which an institution that should be accessible to all, is contaminated by class. Tawney calls for a new ethos in which a decent education is seen as appropriate for all children, regardless of their social position:

> To an educational system which takes as its point of departure,
> not the social conventions of adults, but the needs of children,
> the conventional vulgarities of class and income are merely
> irrelevant. 'A man's education' — to quote the eloquent words

of Professor Nun—'whatever his economic destiny, should
bring him into fruitful contact with the finer elements of the
human tradition, which have been and remain essential to the
value and dignity of civilisation'. What a wise parent, in short,
would desire for his own children, that, and nothing else, it is
our duty to provide to all children. (Tawney, 1924: 5)

Tawney does not confine the school's role to the cultivation of intellectual faculties, stressing that education also has an important part
to play in ensuring the physical well-being of children. He accuses
those who limit the scope of education to mental instruction of ped-
dling 'a piece of inhuman pedantry of which no man would be
guilty in dealing with children of his own' (Tawney, 1924: 8).
Tawney's emphasis on physical health demonstrates his belief that
the effectiveness of education is conditional upon the capacity of
the child to receive it, and that this process is severely retarded if
those fortunate to survive to schooling age are suffering from mal-
nutrition, tooth decay and anaemia. Tawney proposes an eight-
point programme for schools to be utilized as a vital part of public
health (Tawney, 1924: 8–9) — that nursery schools should be
expanded to reduce the defects that currently manifest themselves
during elementary schooling; that specialist schools should be
established to ensure that 'defective' children receive remedial
teaching focused on their individual needs; that the 'mentally
retarded' should be maintained in mainstream schools, but taught
in separate classes with a programme sensitive to their needs; that
open air teaching should be encouraged to combat tuberculosis;
that the physical condition of children should be improved with the
provision of playgrounds; that school trips and camps should be
provided; that adequate school meals should be provided; and that
Local Education Authorities should establish treatment facilities
for illnesses identified by medical inspections.

To put these ideas on education into practice, Tawney proposes a
programme of public expenditure to build more schools and train
and employ more teachers. As in his war essays, he counters
charges of profligacy by employing an opportunity-cost argument,
in which he contrasts the huge amounts spent on a range of rele-
vantly trivial areas, including £400,000,000 on alcohol (Tawney is
presumably referring to consumer spending not government

spending), which could be better spent on education, and he condemns the cabinet that approved cuts in the education budget
(Tawney, 1924: 35; 56). Also, Tawney calls for the abolition of school
fees and the increased provision of maintenance grants by local
authorities (Tawney, 1924: 33–36). Because he recognizes that it was
unrealistic to suggest that this last measure be implemented immediately, in the policy document written for the Labour Party in 1922,
Tawney recommends an increase in scholarships and the expansion of free places as initial steps (Tawney, 1988: 84). In addition, he
argues that the current dependence of working class families on the
wages of their children necessitates the provision of a more gener-
ous maintenance grants to compensate for the reduction in house-
hold income.

With regard to class sizes, Tawney had previously tried to
encourage the reduction of class sizes, but in *Education: The Socialist
Policy*, he devises a coercive framework, suggesting that the Board
of Education should withdraw funding from any establishment
that fails to reduce class sizes to 30 by the end of the decade
(Tawney, 1924: 24). His position on the '11-plus' examination in
which working class children, subjected to rudimentary instruction
in difficult circumstances, are expected to compete with more afflu-
ent students for admittance to secondary schools, had also hard-
ened. Elementary education as a self-contained system would be
abolished, and elementary instruction would become a preparatory
experience for universal secondary education.

> We ought to recognise frankly that up to 18, boys and girls must
> be regarded primarily as future parents and citizens, not as
> wage-earners, and that the proper place for them is not the fac-
> tory, but one type or other of school. The struggle between the
> claims of industry and the claims of health and education,
> which began in 1801, will not be closed, until we have vindi-
> cated the right of the latter to be, at least up to sixteen, the domi-
> nant influence moulding the lives of rising generations.
> (Tawney, 1924: 30)

In the 1922 policy document, Tawney had deprecated the unfair-
ness of a system that discriminates by means of a competitive examination between those children who are, and who are not, most

likely to benefit from a secondary education (Tawney, 1988: 86–87). In the 1924 pamphlet, he adopts a more strident tone:

> Whether a child goes into the mill or continues at school, with all the later consequences which flow from that decision, depends today on the results of a competitive examination taken at the age of 11. To state the situation is to show its absurdity... As far as post primary education is concerned there is only one sound method of selection. It is that *all* normal children should begin some kind of secondary school at the age of 11. (Tawney, 1924: 32)

Freed from a resigned acceptance of the constrictions imposed by formulating the policy of a political party, Tawney is thus able to make the case in much stronger terms for a position that prefigures comprehensive education. Secondary education would be stripped of its class basis and transformed into a universal system of education, which is equally accessible to all, regardless of income.

However, despite this relentless criticism of the vestiges of class privilege, Tawney maintains a remarkable silence about private education. Beyond comments that the term 'Public School' is a comical misnomer, in the policy document, Tawney does not address the issue of private provision because these institutions choose to stand outside the realms of public education (Tawney, 1988: 22). This stance may be understandable in a Labour Party document, where a full assault on private education would have added to the image of red radicalism in a country suspicious of the expansionist ambitions of Bolshevism. But even in *Education: The Socialist Policy*, Tawney remains silent about the private provision of education. This is incongruous not only because of the abhorrence of the class contamination of education that he expresses in this work, but also because of his position in the Diaries where he condemns the provision of education for profit as bordering on blasphemy. However, the only limitation Tawney places on profit-making educational establishments is that they should not receive any public funding. Given that Tawney was fully aware of the capacity of the plutocracy to reproduce itself (hence his advocacy of substantial inheritance tax in *The Acquisitive Society*) it seems odd that the contribution that private education makes to this process is not addressed. It appears that Tawney believed that the universal provision of education would be sufficient to overcome a stratified society, and that the social *cachet* of a private education, not to mention its superior resources and smaller class sizes, would be of little consequence in a functional society. Whatever the truth of the matter, it is certain that Tawney fervently believed that good quality education should be brought within the reach of all children.

For Tawney, therefore, the provision of intellectual and physical education is a right of every child which the government has an obligation to guarantee. Throughout *Education: The Socialist Policy*, published during the early months of Ramsey MacDonald's administration, Tawney refers to the duty of the Labour movement to forge ahead with the programme of educational reform (Tawney, 1924: 5; 6; 12; 46; 54; 57). In a telling remark, Brooks (Tawney, 1988: xiii, xviii–xix), in his introduction to Tawney's *Secondary Education for All*, refers to Tawney's reluctance to propose timescales for the implementation of these educational reforms, but in 1924, freed from the shackles of policy formation, Tawney abandons this caution, setting targets across a range of areas and recommending coercive measures to those institutions which fail to make progress. This strategic opportunism to use power reflects the growing 'politicization' of Tawney's work, indicating how far he has travelled from the often empty platitudes of the *Commonplace Book* that portrayed moral ideals as providing sufficient impetus for change. His engagement with the Labour Party in the realm of policy formation has honed a practical edge that is absent from the Diaries. Having committed himself to equal access, Tawney went on to examine what equality would mean for the school curriculum. His championing of diversity and experiment confounded the socialist stereotype, as we shall now see.

EQUALITY OF NEEDS IN EDUCATION

We have touched on Tawney's belief that educational provision should correspond to the needs of children — in his prescription that their physical and mental needs should be met. Another need to be met is individuality. *The Acquisitive Society*, although a broadly left-wing text, is far from the caricature of socialism as a monolithic system characterized by a drab equality in which diversity is regarded as a form of deviance. Indeed, it depicts the Functional Society as an arena of experimentation with diverse forms of ownership which are judged in terms of their contribution to the creation of an ethical community. This plurality is reflected in the proposals for reform of the educational curriculum which Tawney puts forward in *Education: The Socialist Policy*. Equality should not stifle the shades of individuality that are central to the human condition; an egalitarian education system will accord equal consideration to the unique needs of each student.

When discussing equality in education, one of the main issues is streaming, which involves separating children into different sets according to their perceived ability. Opponents of streaming argue that children in the lower sets who are late developers would not be exposed to the educational stimuli that would allow them to develop to their full potential. This is why a socialist strategy, committed to equality of opportunity, would prefer a single programme experienced by all the pupils. However, for Tawney, equal access should not mean equal treatment for all but equal consideration of individual needs. This entails diversity of educational provision for different pupils in the same school as well as different educational provision in different schools. As Tawney puts it, 'no one should propose that experiment should be sacrificed to any pedantic passion for uniformity' (Tawney, 1921: 59).

From this position, two consequences flow for Tawney: first, there should be a diverse syllabus rather than a standardized national curriculum; and second, there is no need for the state to monopolize the provision of education. On the first proposition, Tawney rejects the notion that a single national curriculum should be imposed — one size does not fit all (Tawney, 1988: 33). The infinite diversity of ideas on the content of educational provision should not be suppressed for the sake of an abstract pursuit of standardization.

The second proposition replicates a central theme of Tawney's political theory — that it is the ends that institutions serve rather than their ownership that matters. As in his theory of property, where diverse modes of ownership can co-exist providing they serve social ends, so with his concept of education, he has no objection to schools being operated by non-governmental organizations, provided that they are not run for profit, and they meet the quality requirements of the Board of Education (Tawney, 1924: 15). The state's proper role is to provide a regulatory framework that establishes broad parameters, not to involve itself in the *minutiae* of daily administration. Schools should be allowed a high degree of autonomy: 'The greater the variety of type among schools, the better, for the need of education is experiment, individuality and the enthusiasm of the pioneer' (Tawney, 1924: 15). This viewpoint reflects Tawney's suspicion of collectivism: he shares the concerns of the guild socialists that a leviathan state, far from being a panacea, would suppress rather than secure human fulfilment. Moreover, given the immensity of the task of ensuring secondary education for all, it would be almost impossible to dispense with the ready-made schools of the voluntary sector, many of which were established for humanitarian reasons.

Tawney's views on education represent his first substantial application of the concept of equality, demonstrating that he has, as a result of his association with the Labour Party, developed a politically aware interpretation of this central socialist value. While there is nothing to suggest that Tawney has abandoned the notion that equality emanates from our equal status in the eyes of God, his entrance into the practical realm of policy means that the concept receives a secular embellishment, which gives it greater practical application. Merely to assert human equality before God does not translate into an egalitarian strategy with specific social initiatives. *Education: The Socialist Policy* demonstrates that Tawney has begun the process of converting the principle of equality into an active force, a tendency that reaches its fullest expression seven years later with the publication of *Equality*. Moreover, this engagement with the Labour Party on educational policy not only stimulated a greater prescriptive element in Tawney's thought, but it led him to examine the development of the Labour movement, which culminated in his greater acceptance of the capacity of secular organizations to craft the moral community he craved. It is to his largely-ignored book, *The British Labour Movement* that we now turn.

4.3 *The British Labour Movement* (1925)

In the *Commonplace Book*, Tawney was disparaging about the
Labour Party for its pusillanimity:

> The rise of the capitalist = the poodle in Faust turning into the
> devil. The Parliamentary Labour Movement = the devil turning
> into the poodle. (Tawney, 1972: 77)

Although this is a cryptic allusion, the inference can be drawn that
Tawney, who strikes an uncompromising tone throughout the Diaries, was condemning what he saw as the timidity of the Party in
asserting the interests of the working class. This attitude is linked to
Tawney's early distrust of the political process and his belief that it
was incapable of generating moral unity because it was mired in the
grubby business of forging alliances with powerful economic
interests.

The British Labour Movement represents a shift away from this
position to a more positive appraisal of the role of political parties
in general and the Labour Party in particular, showing once more
that the Diaries should not be regarded as providing the framework
from which Tawney's subsequent work should be interpreted. The
book arose out of lectures given by Tawney at Yale, and, conscious
that he was delivering them to a foreign audience, and during the
period of the first Labour Government's tenure in office, Tawney is
as much validating the movement with which he is involved as
assessing its history. The opening remarks of the book describe the
seismic shift that had occurred in British politics, in that a party not
connected to the traditional landed interests or the capitalist class is
wielding power for the first time on behalf of the whole nation, with
a doctrine of redistribution and fundamental reform (Tawney,
1968: 1–5). Tawney reassures his American audience, however, that
the radicalism of the Labour movement is confined to its objectives;
its methods were fully within constitutional norms:

> It is not revolutionary in method, because it is confident that it
> can achieve its objects by the use of the ordinary constitutional
> machinery of the country; and, now that it seems to be on the
> verge of winning, it certainly does not intend to alter, or (what
> may in future be more important) to allow other parties to alter,
> the rules of the game. (Tawney, 1968: 5)

But this reassurance is double-edged, because it suggests that the Labour Party's acceptance of democracy is a pragmatic strategy founded on democracy's utility as a mechanism for gaining power, rather than a principle engrained in its philosophy. Such a suggestion once again brings Tawney's commitment to democracy under scrutiny, resurrecting suspicions that his theory has authoritarian implications, even if this was not his intention. However, when Tawney's remark is viewed in the broader context of the book, it becomes clear that he believes that all political doctrines must be legitimated by the House of Commons (Tawney, 1968: 147). In other words, he does not share the Marxist view that representative institutions are a façade because they reinforce ruling class power whilst keeping up the pretence that the interests of all are considered. Tawney stated that 'it [the Labour movement] is the child, not of Marx... but of Robert Owen, of Ruskin and of Morris' (Tawney, 1968: 154). Although he does not rule out the use of violence and direct action, the conditions under which they may be employed are strictly limited: the people should take up arms only if there is an attempt to circumvent parliamentary democracy by disenfranchising elements of the population (Tawney, 1968: 5; 148). Moreover, Tawney affirms the Labour Party's commitment to democratic decision-making in his statement that the 'thousands of members of the party... are well aware that if any serious change is to be made, it requires prolonged discussion and preparation, and that it can be permanent only if based on general consent' (Tawney, 1968: 149).

In *The British Labour Movement* an evolutionary approach is adopted, with piecemeal reform initiated by a democratically elected Labour Party slowly advancing the nation towards a socialist society. Confirming the non-revolutionary credentials of the Labour Party, Tawney emphasizes that there will be no sudden obliteration of class interests, as occurred during the French Revolution (Tawney, 1968: 163). The impatience of the war years, with the urge to harness the benign currents of values flowing from a shared national experience, has metamorphosed into a theory of gradualism, which, though no less trenchant in its abhorrence of social conditions, is a good deal more realistic about the length of the journey to be undertaken.

Tawney divides Labour history into three crucial periods: 1815–1848; 1850–1890; and 1890–1914. The first period was marked by the rise of the proletariat, the formation of the doctrines of Robert Owen and the promising development, but subsequent decline, of Chartism. Discussing the parliamentary approach of the Chartists, Tawney comments that it is typical of the English that 'a band of ragged ruffians should pour its grievances into the parliamentary mould rather than burning factories' (Tawney, 1968: 16). The second period, which is characterized as the golden age of capitalism, saw the working class exhibit a deep distrust of middle class idealism, and form their own defensive organizations which developed into modern trade unions. Trade unions were seen as practical responses to immediate conditions rather than as expressions of abstract philosophies. The third period saw the rise of the Labour Party as a result of increasing governmental reaction against labour organizations. For instance, the trade unions suffered from legislation following the Osborne judgment, which curbed their capacity to act in the interests of their members. Given this interference, it was reasoned that they 'could not afford to leave politics alone', and they actively sought the creation of a political party (Tawney, 1968: 30).

The notion of the Labour movement growing to maturation, recognizing the need to engage in the political process, has parallels with Tawney's own intellectual development. By contrast to the *Commonplace Book*, which lacks an appreciation of the institutional basis of change and exhibits considerable distrust of the political process, *The British Labour Movement* recognizes the need for social organizations to advance the position of the working class, and for the political state to introduce the necessary reforms. Tawney described himself

> as one who has become concerned in labour politics merely for the practical reason that, rightly or wrongly, the particular reforms which appeal to me appeared, without the rise of a Labour Party to the control of public affairs, to have little chance of being realised with reasonable rapidity. (Tawney, 1968: 32)

This statement is significant for two reasons; first, it represents a major enhancement of the role of secular forces within Tawney's politics; second, it raises doubts about the depth of his support for the Labour Party, implying that it may be based on mere expedience (like his earlier characterization of the Labour Party's commitment to democracy). On the first point, examining Tawney's work chronologically reveals an increasing acceptance that political institutions are essential to the development of an ethical society. While commentators agree that Tawney's work during and after the war exhibited a greater institutional realism than in the Diaries, they fail to recognize its full significance. Because their interpretation of the Diaries is bound up with the integral Tawney thesis, they underplay the extent of Tawney's intellectual transformation.

On the second point, Tawney's commitment to the Labour Party may be gauged from the fact that from 1923 to his death in 1962, Tawney was a paid-up member of the Labour Party. However, this is not to deny that he sees weaknesses in the Labour Party. Indeed, he recommends that the Labour Party must avoid an excessive reliance on the trade unions; must reach out of its urban base to rural areas; must build a structure that allows local autonomy to stimulate the grassroots; and must allow policy to be formed by the membership rather than by intellectuals (Tawney, 1968: 37–39; 43; 44). Moreover, the centrality of the Labour Party to Tawney's vision does not entail that the Church cannot operate as a vehicle for change. It can, though it has been deprived of its singular importance, and this means the end of the Tawney's notion of Christian exclusivity.

The British Labour Movement is thus an important work when examining Tawney's intellectual trajectory. It demonstrates that the tendencies that became so apparent in the war essays have culminated in an acceptance of both the capacity of the political realm to contribute to a moral universe, and the centrality of the Labour Party in that process. The movement from a society saturated with the assertion of individual interests, to one in which the morality of fellowship and common ends prevail, is no longer perceived purely in terms of a church propagating the Christian doctrine. Rather it is through the actions of a Labour movement determined to attain power that a moral community can be forged. The secular forces of reform that have come to the fore significantly compromise the

Christian exclusivity of the *Commonplace Book*, necessitating a revision of Tawney's political theory.

4.4 Conclusion

The period 1922–1925 is a highly significant phase in Tawney's development – a significance not given due recognition by the commentaries. Generally, the commentators presents the early Tawney as advocating a thoroughly democratic form of socialism which takes advantage of existing representative institutions, but our developmental analysis shows that this position only becomes fully clarified with the publication of *Education: The Socialist Policy* and *The British Labour Movement*. While it is true that *The Acquisitive Society* (1921) outlines the desirability of an industrial democracy, its lack of discussion about political parties; its declaration that certain classes could be ushered 'politely out of the State',[1] and its framing of common ends in terms of Christianity, raises doubts about the nature of Tawney's democratic commitment. During the period 1922–1925, Tawney deepens his democratic stance by highlighting the role of education in producing a sophisticated electorate capable of choosing the direction the country will pursue. Although it is unclear whether the reform of the education system to cultivate the critical faculties is a pre-requisite for a meaningful democracy, thus delaying the full assumption of responsibilities required in Tawney's Functional Society, *The British Labour Movement* argues that the parliamentary system is adequate to the task of transformation, and that the existing franchise should be defended with physical force if necessary. So it is some nine years after the *Commonplace*

---

1 'We shall secure that such large accumulations as remain change hands at least once in every generation, by increasing our taxes on inheritance till what passes to the heir is little more than personal possessions, not the right to a tribute from industry which, though qualified by death-duties, is what the son of a rich man inherits to-day. We shall, in short, treat mineral owners and absentee landowners as Plato would have treated the poets, whom, in their ability to make something out of nothing and to bewitch mankind with words, they a little resemble, and crown them with flowers and usher them politely out of the State' (Tawney 1921: 104).

Book that we begin to get a comprehensive and clear discussion of democracy by Tawney.

Furthermore, this period is notable for a significant rupture with the Christian exclusivity of the Diaries, when Tawney accepts that the political realm is not bereft of moral content. In the *Commonplace Book*, Tawney was adamant that the absence of a moral ideal within society could only be rectified by an institution which stood above the political morass; this was the Church, animated by its heavenly doctrine. Adopting such a lofty position of a God-loving individual disparaging the impure realm of politics with its unseemly deals and unedifying pursuit of material interests, Tawney could not fully enter the pit of political debate. It is in this context that Tawney's embrace of the Labour Party as the main vehicle of social renewal should be considered.

However, this conversion, as important as it is, should not be cast as a 'road to Damascus' moment, because Tawney's embrace of the Labour Party is an extension of tendencies that became apparent during the war with his recognition of the role of the state in social reconstruction. Equally, it does not indicate that has abandoned his Christian faith or that the Church does not have a contribution to make. He never lost his religious faith, and, as will be demonstrated in the next chapter with *Religion and the Rise of Capitalism*, Tawney continued to accept religion as an important social force. Nevertheless, this change of view is not just a pragmatic realignment as Wright claims, but a fundamental alteration of Tawney's moral doctrine. He is accepting that a predominantly secular organization, with an ideology forged in a moral environment that he previously accused of tainting all within its confines, not only has the capacity to accomplish, but is actually central to, ethical regeneration. A major aspect of Christian exclusivity has been compromised because the Church is not now seen as a sufficient author of moral reformation.

One consequence of this weakening of the Church's role in political reform is that the debate about the meaning of political concepts becomes increasingly secular; indeed, less couched in the language of moral certainty, and more reflective of competing class interests:

> The resounding abstractions which are the conventional and
> somewhat attenuated currency of political controversy —

democracy, liberty, property, justice, equality of opportunity, freedom of enterprise and the rest — however much we may like to regard them as the embodiment of eternal verities, are not like Platonic ideas laid up in heaven, but take their colour and connotations from the dominant interests and practical needs of the different classes which from time to time set the tone of society, and are reinterpreted when, with political and economic changes, those dominant interests undergo a modification. (Tawney, 1968: 11)

The coming struggle will be fought on political terrain, with grand political concepts exemplifying class interests rather than fundamental truths (spiritual certainties). With the publication of his great work, *Equality* (1931), Tawney readdresses the concepts of liberty, duty, egalitarianism and ethics, which had in the Diaries been inextricably linked with his religious beliefs. Before looking at this book, however, it is necessary to examine Tawney's seminal historical work, *Religion and the Rise of Capitalism* (1926).

Chapter Five

Religion and the Rise of Capitalism (1926)

5.1 Introduction

Tawney's contribution to historiography is considerable. The distinguished historian, Hugh Trevor-Roper (1959: 1), characterized the period 1540–1640 as the 'Tawney Century', noting that 'historians who have since studied that period are inevitably, even if unconsciously, affected by his reinterpretation: they can no more think of it now in pre-Tawney terms than sociologists can think of society in pre-Marxist terms'. Tawney's reputation as an historian rests on three seminal works: *The Agrarian Problem in the Sixteenth Century* (1912; see Tawney, 1967), a study of land enclosure; *Religion and the Rise of Capitalism* (see Tawney, 1990), an analysis of the Christian contribution to the development of capitalism and the consequences of economic change on religious dogma; and *The Rise of the Gentry*, which asserts a significant class dimension to the causes of the Civil War. Whilst Tawney's influence is undeniable — his work stimulated a frenetic debate amongst scholars — there were allegations that his use of statistics was dubious (Trevor-Roper, 1959: 4–8), and that his analysis of the period was driven more by his own political commitments and moralistic principles than by a dispassionate attempt to explain the past. Such considerations led another eminent historian, G.R. Elton (quoted in Wright, 1987: 133–134) to describe Tawney's influence as harmful, declaring that he provided erroneous 'grounds for believing that everything that contributed to the greatness and success of their country derived from sinful selfishness and money-grabbing wickedness'.

Beyond the interest it aroused in professional historians, the most important of these works — *Religion and the Rise of Capitalism* — made an impression on lay readers, gaining immense popularity, with sales running into six figures. Moreover, it is Tawney's most intriguing work for those examining his historical works, not for its historical veracity, but for understanding his political thought. It is undeniable that in *Religion and the Rise of Capitalism*, Tawney is less concerned to illuminate the past than to acquire intellectual resources to fight contemporary battles. Tawney is excavating a tradition of Christian thought which imposed moral limitations on economic activities to appeal to the Church to re-engage with the social sphere in order to defeat the crude individualism that has perverted civilized values in England.

In this chapter, our central aim is to assess what bearing *Religion and the Rise of Capitalism* has on the development of the relationship between religion and politics in Tawney's thought. We will find a link between medieval scholasticism and Tawney's notions of Function and avarice; a critique of what he saw as the post-medieval Church's capitulation to the forces of economic development; and an appeal to the modern Church to reverse its historical abdication from the political world, and re-politicize itself with a message of moral renewal.

5.2 Links between medieval scholasticism and Tawney's doctrines of Social Function and avarice

Tawney's intentions in writing his *Religion and the Rise of Capitalism* are clearly expressed from the outset:

> It is to summon the living, not to invoke a corpse, and to see
> from a new angle the problems of our own age, by widening the
> experience brought to their consideration. (Tawney, 1990: 19)

Tawney is studying the past to shed light on the present. In *The
Study of Economic History* (1933) he justifies such an approach,
describing history as the study 'not of a series of events, but of the
life of society'. This is a view which Tawney cultivated in his youth,
when he found the world surprising, and turned to 'history to interpret it' (Tawney, 1978: 54; 48). This does not, however, mean that
Tawney manipulates historical events to cohere with an ideological
narrative for the solution of current problems. On the contrary, he
holds that to achieve an adequate perspective of the present, it is
essential that preceding events are interpreted accurately. So when,
for example, Tawney discusses Christian scholasticism, he does so,
not with the zeal of an advocate, but with the detachment of a
scholar. However, because he also has an eye on the contemporary
relevance of scholasticism, inevitably he is drawn to those elements
which best serve the purpose of guidance.[1]

5.2.1 Social organicism and Social Function

One of these elements—social organicism—bears a close resem-
blance to Tawney's own notion of Social Function:

> Ideally conceived, society is an organism of different grades,
> and human activities form a hierarchy of functions, which dif-
> fer in kind and in significance, but each of which is of value on
> its own plan, provided that it is governed, however remotely,
> by the end which is common to all. Like the celestial order, of
> which it is the dim reflection, society is stable, because it is
> straining upwards. (Tawney, 1990: 34)

Omitting the last sentence, this description of the medieval ideal of
organic society looks very similar to Tawney's concept of a Functional Society outlined in *The Acquisitive Society*, in which distinctions of authority are justified by their contribution to the
all-embracing objective of the social order. It might be argued that

---

1   In seeking guidance from scholasticism on how to solve modern problems, Tawney may
    himself be guilty of Skinner's (1969) mythology of doctrines and/or mythology of prolepsis, by
    projecting roles on to medieval scholastics that they could never have conceived.

the similarities between Tawney's exposition of scholastic organicism and his advocacy of a Functional Society provide credence to the Christian-centric approach to his political works. However, it should not be assumed that Tawney's concept of Function is merely a regurgitation of the medieval Christian notion of organicism. In *The Acquisitive Society* Tawney defines Function in an open manner, as any activity that embodies a social purpose which the agent performs with a sense of responsibility to a higher authority. In that work, the higher authority is the community at large, despite the addition of the final chapter in which Tawney's ideal operates around a Christian society where the Church has a prominent role. It is significant that the idea of Social Function received greatest prominence in the work of Tawney's written during his involvement with the guild movement. So while the idea may take inspiration from pre-industrial society, it is certainly not dependent on religion.

Moreover, Tawney's idea of Function differs from the medieval concept of organicism in his attitude towards the poor. For the medieval schoolmen, the organic interdependence of all classes in society meant that the poor should be protected for reasons of Christian *charity*, whereas for Tawney the poor have a right to decent working conditions and welfare benefits as a matter of humanitarian *justice*. He describes the medieval Church as a giant vested interest, which ignored the injustice of serfdom, and his negative attitude towards those organizations, including contemporary Christian establishments, which speak of assisting the working class in the patronizing tones of charity, is well documented.

Tawney also criticizes medieval organicism for ossifying social life. Scholasticism endorses the notion of a settled, stratified society, in which status is the main determinate of social position, with limited scope for advancement:

> Intellectually, religious opinion endorsed to the full the static view, which regarded the social order as a thing unalterable, to be accepted, not improved. (Tawney, 1990: 68)

By contrast, Tawney's idea of Function, as elaborated in *The Acquisitive Society*, is set in a social system that thrives on the possibility of the talented to advance on the basis of merit, regardless of their class position. It is a dynamic conception employed to generate a transition to an industrious society, characterized by urgency and activity, with the emphasis on humans using their energies to ensure progress.

So, while there are links between medieval organicism and Tawney's notion of a Functional Society, there are important differences between them. Tawney does not slavishly adopt organicism just because it was an integral part of the medieval Christian conception of the social order. The parallels he draws are limited, and strictly on his own terms.

5.2.2 Usury and avarice

Another link between medieval Christianity and Tawney's theory is their shared condemnation of avarice. Central to the scholastic philosophy was the abhorrence of avarice, which expressed itself in the notion of usury (Tawney, 1990: 49–67). This idea, which receives scriptural validation in Exodus, Leviticus and Luke, where it enjoins that those in a position of economic strength should not capitalize on their advantage by charging excessive interest on loans, finds resonance in *The Acquisitive Society*. For instance, Tawney criticizes both shareholders and landowners because of their unjustified extraction of profits from a process to which they made no active contribution. In *Religion and the Rise of Capitalism*, Tawney describes Karl Marx as the last of the schoolmen, following in the footsteps of Henry of Langenstein and St Thomas Aquinas, who castigated the activities of unproductive middlemen and speculators in exploiting the labouring classes (Tawney, 1990: 48).

However, while it is easy to see parallels between Tawney's thought and the medieval doctrine of usury, caution should be exercised before suggesting that Tawney is directly applying the Christian conception, because two factors complicate the picture. First, Tawney does not condemn avarice only because of scriptural injunctions. His argument is based partly on a moral stance that all human beings should expend their energies actively in the economic arena rather than passively benefit from the labour of others; and partly on the practical consideration that economic distortions may occur in a society where a single class extracts a disproportionate amount of national wealth. He claims that the monies appropriated to furnish the personal fortunes of the few had negative economic consequences because there were fewer resources available to reinvest in the development of the economy. These arguments reflect Tawney's general political orientation that concepts should be applied because of their practical usefulness, not merely because of the authority of their derivation. Tawney would occasionally use biblical allusions — not always accurately, according to Dennis and Halsey (1988: 203) — to illustrate an argument, but he rarely regurgitated, or took inspiration from, an idea without some regard to its practical contingencies.

Indeed, Tawney noted that even in medieval times, the social utility of the doctrine of usury was important: 'practical considerations contributed more to the doctrine than is sometimes supposed' (Tawney, 1990: 56). Quoting the notoriously avaricious and scheming Pope Innocent IV, Tawney emphasizes that the medieval prohibition of usury was not merely a distillation of biblical precepts; there was a rational economic case to be made. The widespread practice of usury diverted economic activities away from the essential tasks of the cultivation of land, because the rich ploughed their money into large-scale speculative investments, often resulting in ruin and famine.

Second, religious notions such as 'usury' and 'just price' are always likely to find favour with socialists, not for their derivation or inspiration, but for their role in combatting economic 'vices'. The prohibition of usury conveys the message that the money-lending classes are less worthy than those who actively contribute through their craft, and ensures that the powerful do not dominate the weak by engaging in exhortation. The parallels with socialist conceptions such as the centrality of labour and class exploitation are obvious, suggesting that Tawney's condemnation of avarice draws as much from his socialist sensibility as from any commitment to the medieval Christian scholasticism.

These considerations cast doubt on simplistic interpretations of Tawney's attraction to medieval Christian scholasticism. Given the parallels that can be drawn between Tawney and the critique of capitalism developed by John Ruskin, with the latter's romantic enthusiasm for the pre-industrial order, and Tawney's effusive praise for Elizabethan society contained in the *Commonplace Book*, it might be thought that Tawney entertained a glorified conception of the medieval order. Indeed, in an article which examines the limitations of Tawney's analysis of the market economy contained in *The Acquisitive Society*, Cliff and Tomlinson (2002: 327) argue that Tawney's critique of capitalism rests on a simplistic perception of a 'golden age' in which conduct was guided by religiously-inspired ideas. However, as we have seen, Tawney is more discriminating than this in selecting which scholastic doctrines he is willing to endorse.

5.3 Post-medieval Church's capitulation to economic forces

In his critical account of the Church's record in the post-medieval period, which is the main focus of *Religion and the Rise of Capitalism*, Tawney is much less ambiguous, charting what he believes to be an ignominious retreat of Christianity from the social sphere and the transformation of religious doctrines from outright opposition to the newly emerging economic order, to apologism on its behalf. Human qualities which were regarded as necessary for their contribution to material development were lauded by religion:

> The assertion of economic liberty as a natural right comes at the close of a period in which, while religious interpretation of social institutions was often sincerely held, the supernatural sanction had been increasingly merged in doctrines based on reasons of state and public expediency. (Tawney, 1990: 179)

In the *Commonplace Book*, Tawney had suggested that the Church could operate above the moral morass of society to supply an enlightened ethical ideal. Echoes of this notion are found in the final chapter of *The Acquisitive Society*, where the Church is presented as a vital instrument of change, essential to the attainment of the common ends that characterize a civilized society. In the period between 1921 and 1925, however, Tawney dilutes this notion, by privileging the role of political organizations. With the publication of *Religion and the Rise of Capitalism* in 1926 he goes further, and bit-terly criticizes the post-medieval Church for failing to maintain its moral role against the challenge of industrialization and its atten-dant materialistic ethic. His criticism focuses on two failings—the Catholic Church's organizational corruption; and the Protestant Churches' doctrinal blindness. On the first point, Tawney declares that the Catholic Church's own 'teaching was violated in practice, and violated grossly, in the very citadel of Christendom which pro-mulgated it' (Tawney, 1990: 41). He catalogues acts of papal hypoc-risy and complicity in the Church's pursuit of wealth which compromised the holy teachings on usury and exhortation, refer-ring to the 'notorious corruption of ecclesiastical authorities, who preached renunciation and gave a lesson in greed' (Tawney, 1990: 73). The task of bringing light to the world was undermined because there was a shadow at the supposed source of goodness. This gap between theory and practice was further demonstrated by the failure of the Church to address problems of economic iniquity. The concept of Christian charity, with its concern to protect the weaker members of society, did not translate into a crusade against the worse excesses of serfdom (Tawney, 1990: 70). It was the secular liberal humanitarianism culminating in the French Revolution, not the Catholic Church, which destroyed serfdom.

As for the Protestant Church, Tawney identified the religious doctrines of Lutheranism, Calvinism and Puritanism as successive stages in a religious accommodation with capitalism. Whatever his intentions, Luther's promulgation that there is direct communica-tion between the individual and God devalued the priesthood and man-made religious institutions, culminating in a breach between the soul and society:

> As the soul needs the word alone for life and justification, so it
> is justified by faith alone, and not by any works... Therefore the
> first care of every Christian ought to be to lay aside all reliance
> on works, and to strengthen his faith alone more and more. The
> logic of Luther's religious premises were more potent for pos-
> terity than his attachment to the social ethics of the past, and
> evolved its own inexorable conclusions in spite of them. It enor-
> mously deepened spiritual experience, and sowed the seeds
> from which new freedoms, abhorrent to Luther, were to spring.
> But it riveted on the social thought of Protestantism a dualism

> which, as its implications were developed, emptied religion of
> its social content and society of its soul. (Tawney, 1990:
> 109–110)

Luther's ideas were that the Church and the communion of the
faithful were not essential to the receipt of divine grace. This
encouraged the effective privatization of religion, reducing it from
an active social force scrutinizing economic conduct to a private
quest for salvation. For Tawney, the implications of Luther's ideas
were to set in motion a rationale for the newly emerging acquisitive
society, in spite of Luther's own adherence to key aspects of medieval social organicism. From Luther's unintentional acquiescence
with the new order, Calvinism went a step further in embracing
economic activities, which required capital and credit, and
approved of the cultivation of the economic virtues that contributed to the augmentation of a new material civilization that would,
for Tawney, push morality to the margins (Tawney, 1990: 111–139).
Although Calvin did have an austere streak which condemned
ostentation, his ideas suffered a similar fate to those of Luther, in
that they were developed by his intellectual heirs in a direction that
he would have found objectionable:

> What in Calvin had been a qualified concession to practical exi-
> gencies, appeared in some of his later followers as a frank ideal-
> ization of the life of the trader, as the service of God and the
> training-ground of the soul. (Tawney, 1990: 238)

This deformation which occurred in continental doctrines
expressed itself in the Puritan movement in Britain. Although early
Puritanism promoted virtues that were seen as contributing to economic change, it was fundamentally opposed to material excesses,
and found its core constituency amongst the small master rather
than the rich (Tawney, 1990: 207–213). By the sixteenth century
however, a different strand of Puritanism, which lauded individual
economic effort and enterprise as conducive to the glory of God, tri-
umphed, providing considerable intellectual and practical rationale for the development of an industrial society:

> It was not that religion was expelled from practical life, but that
> religion itself gave it a foundation of granite. In that keen atmo-
> sphere of economic enterprise, the ethics of the Puritan bore
> some striking resemblance to those associated later with the

name Smiles. The good Christian was not wholly dissimilar
from the economic man. (Tawney, 1990: 251)

Tawney criticized the Protestant Church not so much for institutional and personal corruption, as for doctrinal blindness. The Protestants' attraction to the notions of self-help, hard work, tough love,
and the desert principle of justice, led them too readily to identify
with emergent capitalism. Ironically, in its break with the Catholic
Church because of the latter's hypocritical embrace of materialism,
the Protestant Church embraced an ideology — economic liberalism
— which would prove to be a much more powerful organ of materialistic values.

Tawney's belief that religious formulations actively contributed
to the creation and sustenance of capitalism demonstrate not only
that Christianity was an extremely powerful social force, but also
that its meaning can be mangled and transformed by historical contingencies, even from those within its own ranks. The fact that religion bolstered a system which Tawney regarded as irreligious
demonstrates that protestations of divine derivation do not provide
immunity from the deformation of social forces. This conception of
religion as an active social force that can both shape its environment, and in turn be moulded by the conditions in which it operates, is fundamental to Tawney's theory. It provides some hope that
the Church might be able to renew its vision and restore its place as
the upholder of an ethical community by standing up against the
prevailing materialism of the age of capitalism. It is to this aim of
Christian renewal that we now turn.

5.4 The modern Church's attempt at renewal

The first attempt at Christian renewal sought to return to the old
verities of the Church, as a reaction to the materialistic excesses of
the new economic order. However, this move, in its affirmation of
old doctrines, represented little more that a retreat from the attempt
to actively shape reality (Tawney, 1990: 140). The acceptance of a

'pious antiquarianism' reflected the needs of some of the faithful to seek solace in the old certainties by resurrecting the nostrums of medieval scholasticism. But it failed, because its advocates applied a set of ideas that did not appeal to the modern age. One such advocate was Richard Baxter:

> The rules of Christian morality elaborated by Baxter were subtle and sincere. But they were like seeds carried by birds from a distant and fertile plain, and dropped upon a glacier. They were at once embalmed and sterilised in a river of ice. (Tawney, 1990: 225)

Baxter's beliefs were authentic, and his argumentation was strong, but they were dead from their inception because they could not connect with the new order. Tawney's view is that if a 'philosophy of society is to be effective, it must be as mobile and realistic as the forces which it would control' (Tawney, 1990: 155). For Tawney, religion was not primarily a divine revelation that is free from spatial and temporal considerations, but a body of thought that is intimately connected to its period and field of operation. The Church's failure to adapt meant its failure to connect:

> Their practical ineffectiveness prepared the way for their theoretical abandonment. They were abandoned because, on the whole, they deserved to be abandoned. The social teaching of the Church had ceased to count, because the Church itself had ceased to think. (Tawney, 1990: 188)

A biblical exegesis, the acclamation of scriptural authority, and a claim to be the institutional embodiment of a divine doctrine, is not sufficient to ensure wide adherence to a body of social ethics. For ideas to resonate with a social structure they must be seen as realistic and relevant, situated in an adaptive living doctrine that is able to compete in the social market place:

> Their obstinate refusal to revise old formulae in the light of new facts exposed them helpless to a counter-attack, in which the whole fabric of their philosophy, truth and fantasy alike, was overwhelmed together. They despised knowledge, and knowledge destroyed them. (Tawney, 1990: 276)

Tawney's assertion that Christianity needs to adapt itself to new facts demonstrates that he was not protective towards the Christian canon. His acceptance that concessions must be made to revitalize religion as a social force demonstrates that Tawney cannot be identified as a fundamentalist. Although he never denied the continuing relevance of Christian belief, his emphasis is on changing the doctrine to suit the times, rather than revisiting scripture. Tawney's strategy is not to exhume past beliefs, but to concoct a social Christianity that can appeal in contemporary society. This shows that Tawney's Christianity is practical, judged by its capacity to influence and change reality rather than to conform to a pre-established dogma. Religious advocates should reflect on their beliefs, not as an insular exercise in personal salvation, but as a means of making a difference to the lives of their fellow human beings. Tawney evaluates religion, like politics, by its capacity to improve the conditions of the community, a view that became more explicit as his political theory developed. In Tawney's narrative, it is clear that Christianity needs to enter the market place, even if it finds itself side by side on the stall with more tacky goods that often enjoy periods of fashion, to actively compete for the realization of its vision. It is clear from Tawney's historical understanding that the Church must actively engage with the social sphere, changing the nature of its appeal to ensure its continued relevance. This earthier, and un-sanctimonious approach, is further evidence of a move from the Christian exclusivity that pervades Tawney's pre-war musings. Indeed, in *Religion and the Rise of Capitalism*, Tawney seems to reverse the order of priority that he used to hold between religion and politics. In the Diaries, religion is the covert driving force behind Tawney's embrace of a politics of persuasion to ensure social change. But in *Religion and the Rise of Capitalism*, the overriding need for practical reform conditions Tawney's attitude towards religion.

It is true that in urging the Church to re-engage with the social world, Tawney is willing for it to make use of familiar precepts:

> The language in which theologians and preachers expressed their horror of the sin of covetousness may appear to the modern reader too murkily sulphurous; their precepts on the contracts of business and the disposition of property may seem an impractical pedantry. But rashness is a more agreeable failing than cowardice, and, when to speak is unpopular, it is less par-

> donable to be silent than to say too much. (Tawney, 1990: 280–281)

But there is no suggestion here of a slavish adherence or devotion to historical Christian scholasticism. Tawney is not interested in calling on ideas that are outmoded or fail to chime with the times. Rather he wants to apply a spirit of resistance, a critical disposition to an economic civilization that has expelled morality from its sphere, impoverishing human existence and undermining fellowship. *Religion and the Rise of Capitalism* is, therefore, an important contribution to the Tawney project of moral renewal.

5.5 Conclusion

In his *Religion and the Rise of Capitalism*, although he describes some affinity between his doctrine of social function and the medieval Christian concept of social organicism, Tawney makes it clear that religious thought is not immune from the forces of historical change, and that the Church is not protected from critical judgments because of its supposed divine derivation. These clarifications provide further evidence of a shift from the abstract, theoretical formulations of the *Commonplace Book*, to a growing acceptance of the utility of power structures and a more politicized conception of Christianity, driven by an appeal to the modern age. The book is candid in acknowledging the historical abdication of the Church, and appealing for a Christian doctrine that must adapt to circumstances, much like a political ideology. However, as a largely historical work, *Religion and the Rise of Capitalism* does not attempt any serious analysis of political concepts — unlike Tawney's next major book, *Equality*, which many commentators regard as his masterpiece.

Chapter Six

Equality (1931)

6.1 Introduction

With the publication of *Equality* in 1931, Tawney completed the last of the three works (*The Acquisitive Society* and *Religion and the Rise of Capitalism* being the other two) on which his reputation rests. The impact of Tawney's *Equality* has been profound. It has a compelling claim to be regarded as Tawney's greatest, and most respected, work. In his influential study, *Culture and Society 1780–1950* (1958), Raymond Williams (1961: 215; 217), whilst praising *The Acquisitive Society* as 'a fine restatement and revaluation of a traditional case', suggests that *Equality* is more important, as it expands the themes of Arnold, Ruskin and Morris beyond 'moral observation into a detailed and practical argument'. Reviewing the publication of the revised edition of *Equality* in 1952, Barbara Wootton (1952: 266) notes Tawney's pre-eminence in study of social egalitarianism: 'A bibliography of the subject would begin with Tawney 1931 and end with Tawney in 1952'. Indeed, it would not be an exaggeration to claim that the concept of equality is to Tawney what liberty is to John Stuart Mill: for Titmuss (1960: 3) and other Tawney admirers he was the 'apostle of Equality'. Commemorating the centenary of Tawney's birth, Ryan (1980: 410) contrasted the arcane, and eccentric, nature of Tawney's persona and prose with the enduring power of the political appeal expressed in *Equality*:

> The baggy, decaying tweeds (as like as not smouldering, because Tawney had just stuffed a lighted pipe in his pocket), the walrus moustache, the rolling literary style, which showered a working class audience with Latin tags and mysterious references to French playwrights: all these are material for nostalgia and more. [But] The political vision is anything but quaint.

The ideological opponents of British social democracy have also acknowledged the importance of the work: as Honderich (1991: 175) notes, Conservatives 'accord it a kind of respect'. Joseph and Sumption (1979: 2), in their vigorous critique of egalitarianism, describe Tawney's work as an outstanding contribution to the field.

This chapter has three sections. In section 6.2 we discuss Tawney's shift from the concept of equal worth in the Diaries to the concept of equality in the eponymous work. This shift is a move from an exclusively Christian, to an inclusively secular, notion of what it is to be equal. We reject the view of Wright that the shift is a tactical move by Tawney to make his theory more acceptable to a secular audience: in our view, it signifies a fundamental change in Tawney's political theory. In section 6.3, we examine Tawney's elaboration in *Equality* of the content of equality, which he presents as four principles: equality of opportunity; equality of access to basic necessities; equality of consideration; and equality of outcome. We show how he makes use of all four principles in applying his concept of equality to practical policy-making, particularly in his justification of equal educational provision, political equality and industrial democracy. In section 6.4, we consider Tawney's estimate of the prospects for achieving equality, noting his guarded optimism at its gradual extension into the spheres of social welfare, due more to stealth than principle.

6.2 The concept of equal worth

The commentaries in their assumption that Tawney's work displays an underlying consistency, base the Diaries at the centre of the essentialist Tawney thesis, and consider each subsequent work in terms of its contribution to the elucidation of its core political concepts. However, this essentialist approach fails to acknowledge that the spiritual position outlined in the *Commonplace Book* is incompatible with the more secular line adopted in Tawney's published works. This failure is clearly demonstrated with the concept of equal worth, which is accorded particular prominence by Wright:

> There is every reason to regard it as primary. As the evidence
> provided by his *Commonplace Book* clearly revealed, this was the
> inner core of his whole structure of personal and social moral-
> ity, the rock of Christian principle upon which everything else
> was based. In this sense, it was a rock of faith not a philosophi-
> cal argument. It was the expression of religious-based traditions
> of thought about human beings and their worth... Since all men
> were the children of God, each was infinitely precious, an end
> not a means, rich in the possibilities for self-development, broth-
> ers and sisters in a shared humanity and a common civilisation.
> (Wright, 1987: 70)

Wright is thus unequivocal in asserting that equal worth is the core concept on which all of Tawney's subsequent political theory rests and that this is established from the *Commonplace Book*. The difficulty with Wright's argument is that it overlooks the exclusionary basis of the concept of equal worth expressed in the Diaries, where Tawney presents the Christian concept of equal worth as the only sound basis for equality and morality. As Tawney states in the *Commonplace Book*:

> The essence of all morality is this: to believe that every human
> being is of infinite importance, and therefore that no consider-
> ation of expediency can justify the oppression of one by
> another. But to believe this it is necessary to believe in God... It
> is only when we realise that each individual soul is related to a
> power above other men, that we are able to regard each as an
> end in itself. (Tawney, 1972: 67)

The conviction that 'in order to believe in human equality it is necessary to believe in God' demonstrates that, for Tawney, there is an absolute conceptual dependence of the notion of equality on the existence of God. This means that our common ancestry from God is the *only* sound basis for believing in the equal worth of all humans, and mutual obligation and morality are inexorably bound up with this faith-based position. A secular advocacy of equal worth, or a humanist morality, is thus deficient: secular egalitarians who attempt to give a grounding to their theory or define a strategy for equality are hampered by the fundamental philosophical failing that they cannot assert the equal worth of all humans, nor can they find a realistic basis for common humanity because they are incapable of asserting humans' shared inferiority in relation to the Almighty.

However, this is not the argument that Tawney puts forwards in *Equality*. Far from it, Tawney is at pains to emphasize that there is a common egalitarian position that is shared by all progressives, religious and secular, as is shown in his discussion of humanism (Tawney, 1931: 108–114). Tawney notes that many different movements have marched under the banner of humanism, often leading to conflict, but despite this history of division it is an integrative concept that can galvanize the supposed foes against a common enemy.

> So humanism is not the exclusive possession either of those who reject some particular body of religious doctrine or of those who accept it. It is, or it can be, the possession of both... Humanism is the antithesis, not of theism or of Christianity — for how can the humanist spirit be one of indifference to the issues that have been, for two thousand years, the principal concern and inspiration of a considerable part of humanity? — but of mechanism. (Tawney, 1931: 110)

So the various strands of humanism are united on the basis of a common abhorrence to 'mechanism', the principle that the values of the market predominate in societal arrangements. The strands of humanism are characterized by profound commonalities: in Tawney's words, 'they are using different dialects of a common language' (Tawney, 1931: 109). Both religious and secular progressives share divergent aspects of a common conceptual position, which Tawney defines in the following terms:

> Its essence is simple. It is the attitude which judges the externals of life by their effect in assisting or hindering the life of spirit. It is the belief that the machinery of existence — property and material wealth and industrial organisation, and the whole fabric and mechanism of social institutions — is to be regarded as a means to an end, and this end is the growth towards perfection of individual human beings... Its aim is to liberate and cultivate the powers which make for energy and refinement; and it is critical, therefore, of all forms of organisation which sacrifice spontaneity to mechanism... Resting, as it does on the faith that the differences between men are less important and fundamental than their common humanity. (Tawney, 1931: 111)

In maintaining that humanists hold key beliefs in common, Tawney is no longer privileging the religious derivation of the concepts, as he does in the *Commonplace Book*. The position now being advanced is that secular advocates can make a legitimate claim to believe in the equal worth of all human beings, and embrace the concepts that flow from this belief. Wright is not oblivious to this embrace of humanism, commenting that Tawney's revulsion of inequality was not grounded 'merely in his own Christian position. Instead, and interestingly, he invokes the values of a generalised humanism' (Wright, 1987: 43). However, while Wright finds this evocation of humanism interesting, he does not explain why Tawney's adoption of the concept is interesting. Indeed, Wright (1987: 88) later sidelines the concept of humanism, indicating that Tawney's moral case for socialism was 'accurately reflecting its source in his Christian faith (even if sometimes also invoking the support of the moral sensibility of a general tradition of western humanism)'. By relegating Tawney's humanism to a parenthesis, Wright fails to acknowledge the incompatibility between Tawney's early formulation of equal worth and that outlined here in *Equality*. Both the Diaries and *The Acquisitive Society*, with their conviction that the notion of equal worth is necessarily a religious principle, are exclusionary because they question the legitimacy of secular arguments.

In defending his position, Wright's argues that Tawney's later secularistic interpretation of concepts such as equality was merely a tactical move to make his views more palatable to a readership resistant to faith-based arguments. On this view, the intrinsic merits of arguments, which are conceived as within the Christian core, which Tawney holds as a matter of faith, are separated from the social benefits, which are conceived as the attempt to persuade a secular-inclined audience of the utility of his proposals. In other words, Tawney is adopting a twin-track approach, in which his core position is unaffected by his pragmatic appeal to secular progressives; they are merely different arguments, made to produce a similar outcome, which do not collide. However, the suggestion that Tawney suppresses his religious convictions for tactical reasons demeans his integrity. Because the very core of Tawney's theoretical position has altered from the Christian exclusivity of the Diaries, his definition of humanism cannot be merely be seen as a part of a pragmatic exercise in persuasion, but as a fundamental change in his core position. Fifteen years of theorizing and involvement in practical affairs have transformed Tawney's political thought, and the *Commonplace Book* and *Equality* present two different concepts of equality: one is a spiritualized notion of equal worth; while the other is a secularized notion of equality. The differences between the private and published works, therefore, reflect a change of principles; they are not the product of a pragmatic tactic or an idiomatic shift.

6.3 The content of equality

Unlike in the Diaries, in *Equality* Tawney spells out the content and implications of the concept of equality. The concept of equal worth, as Terrill (1973: 128) points out, is vague, in that it 'ruled out certain inhumanities', but begged the question 'what did it positively require?' There is no automatic association between a religious adherence to equal worth and a particular form of egalitarianism. While the concept of equal worth provides us with a powerful argument for not treating humans unequally, it does not tell us what constitutes treating humans unequally. Does it entail equality of

opportunity? Or equality of needs-satisfaction? Or equality of consideration? Or equality of outcome? The Diaries provide no
answers to these questions, but *Equality* does, in its function of
translating the concept of equality into a practical weapon of social
change. We now turn to examine Tawney's treatment of these four
practical criteria of equality.

Before doing so, however, it is worth noting that one general
assumption runs through Tawney's discussion of the four criteria
of equality: positive liberty. Tawney sees no conflict between equality and liberty: indeed, equality is necessary to make a reality of liberty. In the *Commonplace Book*, Tawney briefly, and superficially,
touched on the debate, which was to explode with the publication
in 1958 of Berlin's *Two Concepts of Liberty*, on positive and negative
liberty (Berlin, 2002: 166–218). On that occasion, Tawney stated that
he had no preference between the two, with adoption of either a
matter of expediency. But in *Equality*, he unequivocally embraces
positive liberty:

> a large measure of equality, so far from being inimical to lib-
> erty, is essential to it. In conditions which impose co-operative,
> rather than merely individual, effort, liberty is, in fact, equality
> in action, in the sense, not that all men perform identical func-
> tions or wield the same degree of power, but that all men are
> equally protected against the abuse of power, and equally enti-
> tled to insist that power shall be used, not for personal ends, but
> for general advantage. (Tawney, 1931: 244)

6.3.1 Equality of opportunity – to each according to their talents

Of the four concepts of equality discussed by Tawney, the notion
that all should have an equal chance of progression on the basis of
their talents might seem to be, on the face of it, the least controver-
sial, gaining wide assent across the political spectrum. Tawney
himself appears to be highly sympathetic towards it, arguing that
espousing a concept of equality did not mean asserting that everyone is the same, but rather that we should reduce social inequalities
which have nothing to do with the natural differences between
people:

> So to criticize inequality and to desire equality is not, as some-
> times suggested, to cherish the romantic illusion that men are

> equal in character and intelligence. It is to hold that, while their
> natural endowments differ profoundly, it is the mark of a civil-
> ised society to aim at eliminating such inequalities as have their
> source, not in individual differences, but in its own organisa-
> tion, and that individual differences, which are a source of
> social energy, are more likely to ripen and find expression if
> social inequalities are, as far as practicable, diminished.
> (Tawney, 1931: 63)

This statement suggests that for Tawney, people are entitled to reap
the rewards for their different talents. While discrimination on the
grounds of institutionally entrenched inequalities is unacceptable,
discrimination on grounds of natural differences is legitimate.
Moreover, meritocracy is socially valuable:

> a community must draw on a stream of fresh talent, in order to
> avoid stagnation, and that, unless individuals of ability can
> turn their powers to account, they are embittered by a sense of
> defeat and frustration. The existence of opportunities to move
> from point to point on an economic scale, and to mount from
> humble origins to success and affluence, is a condition of social
> well-being and of individual happiness, and impediments
> which deny them to some, while lavishing them on others, are
> injurious to both. (Tawney, 1931: 143)

However, the concept of equality of opportunity arouses controversy in left-wing circles because of its close association with market economies, where the emphasis is on the importance of the
competitive struggle as a means of generating a dynamic and productive social system. Indeed, it has been doubted whether the idea
should be admitted into the egalitarian family at all, given that it
appears to place no restrictions on the development of a highly
stratified society (Baker, 1996: 46–47; Barry, 1989: 175). Tawney
himself certainly saw the principle of equality of opportunity in
terms of market economics, and Terrill (1973: 123) is correct in
asserting that Tawney appreciated the worth of the notion to the
extent that it contributed to the rationale that helped to remove the
constrictions imposed by the feudal order. Parallels can be drawn
with Tawney's approval of liberal philosophy in *The Acquisitive
Society* for removing the legal impediments that stymied individual
powers and prevented economic development. However, Tawney
pointed out that just as the promotion of the market mechanism

degenerated from a principle of liberation to one of repression, so the doctrine of equality of opportunity became the basis for new forms of inequality:

> It had not attacked all forms of inequality, but only those which had their roots in special advantages conferred on particular groups by custom and law. It was not intolerant of all social gradations, but only of such as rested on legal privilege. The distinctions of wealth and power which survived when these anomalies had been removed, it surrounded with a halo of intellectual prestige and ethical propriety. It condemned the inequalities of the feudal past; it blessed the inequalities of the industrial future. (Tawney, 1931: 135–136)

The problem with equality of opportunity in its historical manifestation is that it was a partial idea, connected with the liberation of a particular class. In helping to overcome the dead hand of the aristocracy, it established a plutocracy which was equally determined to maintain its privileged position. It is noticeable in Tawney's discussion that he does not challenge the basic notion of the concept that each should have the capacity to rise as his or her talents justifies. Rather, he objects to the notion becoming perverted into a form of ideology, or, in one of Tawney's stock phrases, the 'decorous drapery', which hid the harsh facts of a new form of subordination. The illusion of a society in which each are free to ascend according to their abilities, where equality of opportunity is 'encouraged to reign as long as it does not rule', provoked Tawney's famous tadpole analogy:

> It is possible that intelligent tadpoles reconcile themselves to the inconveniences of their position, by reflecting that, though most of them will live and die as tadpoles and nothing more, the more fortunate of the species will one day shed their tails, distend their mouths and stomachs, hop nimbly on to dry land, and croak addresses to their former friends on the virtues by means of which tadpoles of character and capacity can rise to be frogs. (Tawney, 1931: 142)

The faint possibility of exceptional individuals from the lower class rising to the higher class can be distorted to put a meritocratic gloss on a system whose fundamental inequality ensures that the great mass of the population are unable to fully develop their talents. It is against this picture of widespread social exclusion that the idea of equality of opportunity needs to be assessed. Whilst the basic principle of equality of opportunity — that individuals should occupy a position in society that reflects their ability — is sound, Tawney contends that it has suffered an historical deformation, in that the capacity to rise is conditioned by the social position of the individual. The working classes have not had access to adequate healthcare; have been allowed to languish in poor housing; and have been denied a full education. The nature of social conditions ensures that equality of opportunity is reduced to a justificatory platitude for a class system in which most individuals are not afforded the opportunities to make the best of their endowments:

> But, in the absences of measures which prevent the exploitation of groups in a weak economic position by those in a strong, and make the external conditions of health and civilisation a common possession, the phrase equality of opportunity is obviously a jest, to be described as amusing or heartless according to taste. It is the impertinent courtesy of an invitation offered to unwelcome guests, in the certainty that circumstances will prevent them from accepting it. (Tawney, 1931: 150)

It is clear, therefore, that the prospect of social mobility promised by equality of opportunity becoming reality depends 'not only upon an open road, but upon an equal start' (Tawney, 1931: 143). To answer the question of how to ensure that everyone gets an equal start, Tawney turns to the next concept of equality — equality of needs-satisfaction.

6.3.2 Equality of access to basic necessities — to each according to their needs

For Tawney, a pre-requisite of equality is that everyone's basic natural or human needs should be met:

> Nature, with her lamentable indifference to the maxims of philosophers, has arranged that certain things, such as light, fresh air, warmth, rest, and food, shall be equally necessary to all her children, with the result that, unless they have equal access to them, they can hardly be said to have equal rights, since some will die before the rights will be exercised, and others will be too enfeebled to exercise them effectively. (Tawney, 1931: 193)

Note that Tawney is calling for equal access to the physical necessities of life, not equal outcomes such as equal health: 'it is possible to secure to all, not equal health, but an environment equally favourable to its preservation' (Tawney, 1931: 199). Equal access implies that all human beings, regardless of their social position, should live in conditions that are conducive to the attainment of a basic standard of living. Employing a raft of statistics, Tawney shows that Britain's unequal social structure was responsible for making disease and premature death a widespread feature of working class life (Tawney, 1931: 192–199). These afflictions are not the product of nature, but the result of social conditions that can be removed:

> For, if health is purchasable, it is also expensive, and for the mass of mankind its conditions must be created by collective action, or not at all. (Tawney, 1931: 196)

Moreover, education is included in Tawney's conception of human needs: after our physical needs have been met, education is necessary to provide the enrichment required to create and sustain a civilized society. In *Equality*, Tawney follows the arguments presented in his pamphlet *Education: The Socialist Policy* in deploring the contemporary class dogma that sees the working class as less worthy of a good education than those from a more prosperous background.

However, for Tawney, equality of access to basic necessities does not mean identical provision for all. Everyone's needs are different, so they should be addressed differently. This brings us to Tawney's third concept of equality — equality of consideration.

6.3.3 Equality of consideration – to each according to their 'idiosyncrasies'

Given Tawney's enthusiastic embrace of the individuality of each human being, or as he preferred to put it, 'the charm of their varying idiosyncrasies', it is natural that this would translate into a conviction that these differences should be nurtured rather than obliterated (Tawney, 1931: 63–64):

> equality of provision is not identity of provision. It is to be achieved, not by treating different needs in the same way, but by devoting equal care to ensuring that they are met in different

> ways most appropriate to them, as is done by a doctor who pre-
> scribes different regimens for different constitutions, or a
> teacher who develops different curricula. The more anxiously,
> indeed, society endeavours to secure equality of consideration
> for all its members, the greater will be the differentiation of
> treatment which, when once their common needs have been
> met, it accords to the special needs of different groups and indi-
> viduals among them. (Tawney, 1931: 51–52)

A potential problem with Tawney's notion of equal consideration is that it could be used to justify discrimination. For example, the seg-regation policy adopted by white racists in the USA was justified on grounds that it delivered 'equal but different' provision to black people. In Tawney's own usage of the concept, the charge that very unequal results can be generated by applying equal consideration could be brought against his analysis of educational provision, because he establishes the principle of equal consideration for all within education without elaborating how this would work in prac-tice: he offers no guidance on what criteria should be employed when deciding to apply a particular educational regime to a child. Given his advocacy of a decentralized structure in which schools have a great deal of flexibility in determining policy providing they remain within the broad guidelines of the Board of Education, there is a danger, notwithstanding Tawney's intentions, that unequal provision could be the result.

Tawney appears to deal with this danger in his assertion that all children in a community should go to the same schools:

> The English educational system will never be, what it should
> be, the great uniter, instead of being, what it has been in the
> past, a source of disunion, until children of all classes of the
> community attend the same schools. (Tawney, 1931: 204)

This statement reflects Tawney's desire to end segregation in soci-ety by removing divisions nurtured by a school system arranged along class lines. His preference is for schools that reflect a broad social mix to establish a basis for mutual understanding and ulti-mately a harmonious society. He is not calling for a monolithic school system, but a varied school structure with a diverse intake. However, he undermines this statement by tolerating the continuation of the system of private education when he makes the following remark:

> Special schools for the rich, if they still survive, will form one minor category within the national system, offering curative treatment, perhaps, to such children as require it. (Tawney, 1931: 205)

Although he seeks to play down the implications of this concession by implying that the number of private schools would be few, it undermines his egalitarian principle in education. Employing the irony that is a prominent feature of his work, Tawney's reference to 'curative treatment' almost suggests that he regards the rich, who want to opt out of the universal system of education, as a suitable case for treatment. Moreover, Tawney does not condemn the private provision of healthcare; he is more concerned to press for collective action to remove the most chronic healthcare deficiencies that plague working class life.

6.3.4 Equality of outcome

The first three concepts of equality discussed by Tawney are procedural rather than substantive principles, in that they are designed to secure a just process for the delivery of certain goods, rather than the direct delivery of the goods themselves. So equality of opportunity means ensuring that no artificial obstacles stand in the way of a person taking advantages of their talents, rather than providing particular opportunities to them. Similarly, equality of access to basic necessities means removing barriers (such as poverty) to obtaining food, shelter, health care and education, not the allocation of those goods themselves. Likewise, equality of consideration means creating a system that responds to the different characteristics that people have, rather than assuming that one size fits all. However, Tawney also discusses a substantive concept of equality — equality of outcomes.

Equality of outcomes is important to Tawney, less in the sense of prescribing an equal distribution of goods than in the sense of limiting the extent of an unequal distribution. He is especially anxious to prevent the concentration of economic *wealth*, and the concentration of economic *power*, in too few hands. On economic *wealth*,

Tawney is perfectly prepared to see people being rewarded differen-
tially for work of different value:

> No one thinks it is inequitable that, when a reasonable provi-
> sion has been made for all, exceptional responsibilities should
> be compensated by exceptional rewards, as recognition of the
> service performed and an inducement to perform it. For differ-
> ent kinds of energy need different conditions to evoke them,
> and the sentiment of justice is satisfied, not by offering every
> man identical treatment, but by treating individuals in the same
> ways, in so far as, being human, they have requirements which
> are the same, and in different ways in so far as, being concerned
> with different services, they have requirements which differ.
> (Tawney, 1931: 154)

In previous works, Tawney had viewed gradations of pecuniary
reward as justified by the differential worth of the service rendered
to the community, with individuals motivated by a principle of
social service, though rewarded only so much as to allow them to
continue performing that important social function. Although the
notion of inducement was not discussed then because it was a form
of self-interest that stretched the parameters of Tawney's austere
early theory, in *Equality* he is more comfortable with inducements,
though he clearly wants basic needs ('a reasonable provision... for
all') to be met before inducements can be considered.

However, there are limits to the extent of inequality of wealth
that Tawney is willing to accept, and the current distribution is well
beyond that limit. Accordingly, he holds that the income of the poor
should be increased and the wealth of the rich should be reduced
(Tawney, 1931: 35). In previous works, he describes excessive
wealth as immoral, particularly when contrasted with the extent of
deprivation, and he also rather quaintly describes it as ungentle-
manly in *The Acquisitive Society*. In *Equality*, he regards the extremes
of wealth and poverty as anti-social and degrading, souring social
relations with servility and resentment on the one hand, and
patronage and arrogance on the other (Tawney, 1931: 35). So the
gap between rich and poor needed to be reduced in order to produce a cohesive society in which all citizens were within reach of
each other. Reducing income disparities tackled social exclusion
from two directions: alleviating the poverty of the working class;

and limiting the capacity of the middle and upper classes to opt out of social intercourse.

In answer to the question of what method of economic redistribution to adopt, Tawney reiterates his belief that large incomes should be subject to substantial death duties and progressive taxation. The fortunes bequeathed by the rich belong to the class-based society and have no place in Tawney's egalitarian society. However, such measures did not mean a direct money transfer to the poor, because a direct monetary transfer would yield very little in terms of additional funds for working class families (Tawney, 1931: 166–168). Tawney viewed crude monetary reallocation as a policy that no one on the left actually advocated: it was a myth fostered by right-wing critics to simplify their task of criticizing socialism:

> Equality is to be sought, not by breaking into fragments the large incomes which are injurious both to those who receive them and to those who do not, but by securing that an increasing proportion of the wealth which at present they absorb will be devoted to purposes of common advantage. (Tawney, 1931: 172)

By 'common advantage', Tawney here means the development of social capital, by nurturing institutions which make available to everyone the means of civilization, and by fostering the type of social relationships that reinforce human fellowship. So the produce of redistribution would be invested in the communal provision of health care, housing and education to meet those basic needs that ensure everyone has the means to grow and develop and interact with their fellows on a basis of mutual respect. As we noted in chapter three, in the final chapter of *The Acquisitive Society* (1921: 227), Tawney perceived the devotion to common ends as a religious principle that is best promoted by the Church. But in his later works, he interprets the common advantage as a secular concept, which will be obtained not by the sermons of the street corner preacher identified in the Diaries, nor by the proselytizing Christian Church which is given such a prominent role in *The Acquisitive Society*, but by the operation of social institutions guided by the democratic political apparatus. This is expressed in Tawney's advocacy of generalized humanism, and is neatly summarized when he outlines and commends Matthew Arnold's and John Stuart Mills' interpretations of the meaning of equality:

> in spite of their varying characters and capacities, men possess in their common humanity a quality which is worth cultivating, and that a community is most likely to make the most of that quality if it takes it into account in planning its economic organisation and social institutions — if it stresses lightly differences of wealth and birth and social position, and establishes on firm foundations institutions which meet common needs, and are a source of common enlightenment and common enjoyment. (Tawney, 1931: 61)

On preventing the concentration of economic *power*, Tawney notes that the concept of power has traditionally been discussed in relation to political authority, while its operation within the economic system has been confined to the margins (Tawney, 1931: 228). But, a modern industrial society, which Tawney believes is concentrating ownership amongst an ever-decreasing number of enterprises, necessitates an analysis of economic power. With the advent of universal suffrage, the battle for political equality may be over, but the battle for economic power was just beginning:

> The extension of liberty from the political sphere, where its battle, in most parts of Western Europe, is now, perhaps, won, to those of economic relations, where it is still to win, is evidently among the most urgent tasks of industrial communities, which are at once irritated and paralysed by the failure to effect it. (Tawney, 1931: 243)

The democratization of economic structures is, therefore, an essential task for progressive forces. Current power relationships within the economy are not founded on legitimate authority, but on sheer economic might. As Tawney memorably states: 'freedom for the pike, is death for the minnows' (Tawney, 1931: 238). The predatory nature of capitalism, where enterprises wield power on the basis of elite, not democratic, decision- making, means that the interests of private individuals are being privileged over the public interest. For Tawney, such exercise of economic power was arbitrary, imperilling the democratic basis of the country, and consigning the great mass of the population to the precarious position of dependence on the whims of the capitalist. It is a vital part of Tawney's

equality agenda, therefore, to legitimize economic power by mech-
anisms that transfer control over it to the wider community.

Some of Tawney's prescriptions replicate those elaborated in *The
Acquisitive Society*, although the influence of guild socialism has
waned. He imposes three conditions on the exercise of economic
power: it should be exercised for social purposes approved by the
community; it should be no more extensive than is required to serve
social purposes; and it should be revocable if it is used in an arbitrary
manner. These principles translate into a practical programme for
bringing the commanding heights of the economy into public control, through a mixture of regulation and nationalization. Greater
responsibility should be devolved to workers through their trade
unions, who would hold joint discussions with the management
and be fully consulted about the future direction of the firm. Plans
for nationalization should be submitted to a standing industrial
committee, to ensure that every effort is made to minimize the
social cost, while in larger industries, matters related to profits, the
power of directors, and relations with the consumer will be governed by rules established by a public department (Tawney, 1931:
261–282).

So Tawney's concept of equality of outcome is wide-ranging,
covering disparities of both wealth and power in economic affairs.
His analysis of it complements his analyses of the other three concepts—equality of opportunity; equality of access to basic necessities; and equality of consideration—to provide a comprehensive
account of the notion of equality, together with prescriptions on
how to implement it. Tawney's understanding of equality is no longer constrained by the exclusionary Christian basis of his early
advocacy of equal worth, nor by his previous belief that the common ends are essentially a religious principle which should be
propagated by the Christian Church. Rather he is propounding a
theory that sees social institutions guided by the democratic norms
of a political democracy as the cement of a society founded on fellowship. Tawney notes that recent changes in society have brought
the prospect of achieving equality closer: these changes are examined in the next section.

6.4 The prospect for equality

Echoing Matthew Arnold, Tawney appeals to the populace to choose equality. It is a hallmark of his political theory that the direction of society is not determined by the operation of social forces or inexorable laws of development, but by the preferences and values of human beings. However, since the First World War, Tawney tones down the extent of his belief in the power of ideas to transform society. In the *Commonplace Book*, he set out a position which implied that the dissemination of ideas was largely responsible for the pre-war unrest that dogged the liberal government. Even when Tawney produced *The Acquisitive Society*, which displays a greater institutional awareness, the guild socialist A.R. Orage described him as the man who 'believed capitalism would capitulate to reasoned argument' (quoted in Hutchinson and Burkitt, 1997: 97). But while it is true that throughout his life, Tawney placed considerable faith in the power of ideas, in *Equality* there is a shift towards Fabianism in accepting that there has been a structural move towards egalitarianism in which the intentions of humans have played only a limited role.

Tawney believes that since the end of World War I there has been progress towards a more humane society, as evident in the continuing expansion of social services and industrial legislation. This is despite the fact that public opinion in Britain continues to regard the abstract concept of equality as anathema, a continental curiosity, wholly out of kilter with the British national temperament:

> while protesting that nothing is further from their minds than to be lured, like France in the past, or Russia to-day, by the egalitarian mirage, they have permitted themselves to make fitful and circuitous approaches towards it. Without ceasing to gaze, in a bold, dignified manner, in the opposite direction, they have stumbled, in spite of their principles, into the employment of a technique, by which the impractical can, when they so desire, in some measure be performed, and by which some kinds of inequality have, in fact, been diminished. (Tawney, 1931: 165)

The development of the industrial society increased the aggregate wealth of the nation, but initially concentrated this wealth in the hands of privileged few, denying a decent existence to the majority of the population. The advent of political democracy 'with the grad-ual extension of the franchise' has meant that the demands of this majority had to be reckoned with (Tawney, 1931: 174), and this has led to some interventionist measures taken by the state on a piece-meal, tactical basis. Taken together, these uncoordinated, prag-matic interventions have promoted the cause of equality. So although equality as an abstract principle has not been adopted either by the governing class or by the populace at large, the defor-mation of the social fabric has compelled the taking of measures that are contributing to this objective. Tawney's approval of a frag-mented advance towards equality marks a contrast with *The Acquisitive Society*, which, with its imagery of the broken ends of industry, gave the impression that the collapse of capitalism was imminent unless the English abandoned their distrust of abstract principles and embraced the values of a Functional Society. This change in his thought indicates that Tawney's political orientation had taken a further turn towards Fabianist gradualism. Signifi-cantly, *Equality* was dedicated to Sydney and Beatrice Webb.

6.5 Conclusion

In this chapter on Tawney's masterpiece, *Equality*, we have traced his mature views on the most important concept in his political the-ory. We have shown how his analysis of equality releases it from the exclusivist Christian straitjacket of the Diaries to embrace an inclusivist secular framework. This is not a tactical move by Tawney to curry favour with a more secular public, but a funda-mental reorientation of his political thought towards universalism. Alongside this shift, for the first time Tawney elaborates the sub-stance of equality, explaining its practical application in terms of four principles — equality of opportunity; equality of access to basic necessities; equality of consideration; and equality of outcome. All of these principles play a part in Tawney's vision of a just society in which everyone is entitled to a minimum standard of material well-being, as well as to educational provision and political and industrial democracy. Tawney believes that such a vision is not unrealistic — indeed it is already being realized, if in a piecemeal, pragmatic way because of the English aversion to abstract principles such as equality.

Although the next (and last) three decades are relatively quiet for Tawney, he does produce some works that shed further light on his political thought. While he had already completed his most significant works, the following period sees him make changes that take him further away from the Christian basis of the Diaries. He explores the role of political parties in assisting the development of socialism; he embraces the liberal doctrine of rights; and he tempers his austere version of liberty. We turn to these discussions in chapters 7 and 8.

Chapter Seven

Tawney's Essays Between 1934 and 1937

The Choice Before the Labour Party (1934); A Note on Christianity and the Social Order (1937)

7.1 Introduction

The period after the publication of *Equality* is generally regarded as a barren time for Tawney, because his intellectual output fell significantly. By contrast to the decade 1921–1931, which was marked by the publication of his three great works, the next 31 years would generate only two books, one of which is a study of China (1937) that is marginal to our concerns; and the other a pedestrian historical work on the life of the merchant and minister, Lionel Cranfield (1958). The trenchant literary style, that was as much a mark of Tawney's political thought as were his prescriptions, had by the late 1930s lost some of its verve, often appearing cumbersome and opaque, with only occasional flashes of brilliance. Terrill (1973: 139), commenting on the decline in Tawney's productivity, argues that the political context of the thirties, which was a high watermark in socialist theorizing, left Tawney bewildered, unable to make an impact on the public scene: 'Tawney was depressed, and intellectually a bit paralysed by the intensifying concentration of irresponsible governmental power and the rise of totalitarian ideologies all over Europe.'

However, whilst there is clearly a drop in output and literary vivacity, this does not undermine the significance of the interventions that Tawney did make during the remainder of the 1930s, dealing with issues which he had hitherto neglected, and exploring further the connection between religion and society. This chapter will first examine his 1934 essay, *The Choice Before the Labour Party*, where he reflects on the purpose of the Labour Party after the defection of Ramsay MacDonald and the cataclysmic election defeat of 1931. Second, in section 7.3, we deal with Tawney's 'religious' essay, *A Note on Christianity and the Social Order*, which, while not marking a return to the reductive Christian exclusivity of the Diaries, shows that religious doctrine remains an important, if now subordinate, dimension of his thought.

7.2 *The Choice Before the Labour Party* (1934)

The Choice Before the Labour Party is Tawney's first sustained engagement with the purpose of the Labour Party in relation to its membership and the achievement of socialism. This is a significant issue, because Tawney's contribution to the Labour Party is one of the defining elements of his political project. Although his influence has sometimes been exaggerated — as by Geoffrey Foote (1985: 80) in claiming that Tawney's contribution cannot be 'over-estimated', and by Dennis and Halsey (1988: 149) in their excessively reverential discussion of Tawney in *English Ethical Socialism*, remarking that he has been a 'source of exemplary wisdom for the Labour Party for forty years' — hidden amongst the hyperbole there is a kernel of truth.

Tawney's essay was provoked by the so-called 'Great Betrayal' of 1931. The Labour Prime Minister, Ramsey MacDonald, requested

an audience with the King to tender the resignation of an administration that had been battered by the repercussions of the Wall
Street Crash and the orthodoxy that the value of the pound should
be linked to the gold standard. The government had been strongly
advised to introduce a policy of financial retrenchment which
included cuts in unemployment benefits, but such a policy was
unconscionable to a government elected to advance the socialist
cause, and the cabinet took the decision to resign from office. To
general astonishment, however, MacDonald returned from his
meeting with the King as Prime Minister of a predominantly Conservative National Government. The descent of MacDonald into
Labour demonology is one which reverberates to this day, reflecting the hatred felt by the Labour Left towards any leader who is
perceived to be ideologically suspect or willing to entertain the
ideas of the Tory class enemy. This is, as Pimlott (1992: 496) puts it
in his biography of Harold Wilson, 'the spectre which always
haunted Labour leaders' when problems descend. This harrowing
and defining moment for the Labour Party provides the background for a forthright appraisal by Tawney of the purposes of the
Labour Party, which represents a further development of his political theory.

In the post-mortem on the Great Betrayal, the event was widely
interpreted as a personal betrayal by MacDonald, who was castigated as a traitor, willing to sacrifice his party for the retention of
power. He has been portrayed as a vain man, easily seduced by flat-
tery and the prospect of receiving plaudits from the rich. However,
Sassoon (1997: 63), in his magisterial study of Western European
socialism in the twentieth century, explains how this mantra of
treachery prevented a proper appraisal of the problems of the
Labour Party: 'The only explanatory category which was used was
that of "betrayal": Labour failed to advance towards socialism
because it was betrayed by its leaders — MacDonald and Snowden.
This explanation, by ascribing the sole responsibility for the Labour
rout 1929–1931 to its leaders, prevented further thought.' Sassoon's
claim that the real cause of the Labour Party's demise was its internal policy failure, not the character of its leader(s), is the starting
point of Tawney's analysis. Referring to the judgment of an ordinary citizen, Tawney declares that:

> It is possible that his verdict on its death, if at this time of day he
> paused to consider it, would be neither murder nor misadven-
> ture, but pernicious anaemia producing general futility. For the
> events of 1931 were the occasion rather than the cause of the
> *debacle* of the Labour Party. (Tawney, 1953: 52)

Tawney argued that it was dishonest to look for scapegoats:

> If the laments of some ex-minister at the 'conspiracy', which
> 'stabbed them in the back' — as though a Titan, all energy and
> ardour, had been felled at his forge by the hand of assassins —
> were merely undignified, they would probably be ignored.
> Unfortunately they are worse. What Labour most needs is not
> self-commiseration, but a little cold realism... They retard the
> recovery of the party by concealing its malady. They perpetuate
> the mentality which requires to be overcome before recovery
> can take place. The sole cure for its disease is sincerity. They
> offer it scape-goats. (Tawney, 1953: 54)

It was the conduct of the party in power that secured its fate,
because it was prepared to sacrifice its principles to the retention of
power rather than use power to promote its principles. As Tawney
sarcastically remarks, 'His Majesty's Labour Government could
rival the most respectable of them in cautious conventionality'
(Tawney, 1953: 53). Until it is accepted by its critics that the problem
was the Labour Party's failure to follow the fundamental socialist
principles that distinguish it as a radical political force, then the
process of re-building cannot begin. In section 7.2.1, Tawney's conception of a political creed is elaborated to show the continuing primacy of principles in altering political reality, and section 7.2.2
shows that Tawney's explanation for the absence of political principles in the Labour Party is that its programme for government is
more about responding to sectional groups within the Party than
about the way to create a classless society.

7.2.1 The priority of principles

For Tawney, a political creed is made up of agreed principles of
action, based on the fundamental needs of human beings:

> A political creed, it need hardly be said, is neither a system of
> transcendental doctrine, nor a code of rigid formulae. It is a
> common conception of the ends of political action, and of the

> means of achieving them, based on a common view of the life
> proper to human beings and the steps required at any moment
> more nearly to attain it. (Tawney, 1953: 56)

Tawney sees its political creed as a pivotal element in the Labour
Party, because it determines its political programme and is central
to its aim of attracting the allegiance of the electorate. Indeed, without a firm ideological anchorage, the Party would be divided on
key issues and uncertain of its destination. The official creed of the
Labour Party is socialism, but the tragedy of the Party is its failure
to conceive its actions in terms of its ideology:

> The inner state of the movement has been concealed from itself
> by the glamour of the word. That word is Socialism. In 1918, the
> Labour Party, finally declared itself to be a Socialist Party. It
> supposed, and supposes, that it thereby became one. It is mis-
> taken. (Tawney, 1953: 58)

The appellation of a label is not sufficient to characterize a party; the
organization must demonstrate its commitment by acting in accordance with the principles which constitute its doctrine. The Labour
Party has acted under the misapprehension that its rhetorical commitment to the doctrine sufficiently defines its being. But the evidence of the last government, with its willingness to compromise to
remain in power, demonstrates that the Party has not translated its
professed principles into practice. The 1924–1925 Labour Government's lack of genuine commitment to its creed produced policy
inertia, as the preservation of power became its main operating priority (Tawney, 1953: 53; 55), and the 1929–1931 Labour Government
has failed for the same reason.

Tawney argues that socialism, like all radical creeds, consists of
three integral components that must be adhered to if the political
organization is to function in accordance with its principles
(Tawney, 1953: 58). First, it must have a common conception of the
society it wishes to create. Second, it must devise ways of overcom-
ing the resistance that will follow efforts to create the desired community. Third, it must agree on the machinery needed to
operationalize the new order. Tawney asserts that British Socialism
has devoted considerable time to the third factor, but insufficient
time to the other two factors. The Labour Party has not performed
the:

> painful necessity of clarifying its mind, disciplining its appe-
> tites, and training for a tough wrestle with established power
> and property. It touched lightly on its objectives, or veiled them
> in the radiant ambiguity of the word Socialism, which each
> hearer could interpret to his taste. So it ended by forgetting the
> reason for its existence. It has now to rediscover it. (Tawney,
> 1953: 60)

The ideology of socialism has not provided the Party with direction: indeed it has served as a convenient term to disguise the lack
of a common conception of the Party's enterprise. The term 'socialism' has operated as an iconic symbol, adopted to give the appear-
ance of unity amongst disparate factions which are divided by
discrete doctrines that have diverted the Party from devising a
principled programme to give direction to their cause. Tawney
demands that the Party thinks about its principles in a way that is
practical enough to translate into a programme that will attract
electoral support. He outlines the guiding objective of the Labour
Party that should animate the activities of all members:

> The fundamental question is, as always: Who is to be the mas-
> ter? Is the reality behind the decorous drapery of political
> democracy to continue to be economic power wielded by a few
> thousand—or, if that be preferred, a few hundred thousand—
> bankers, industrialists, and landowners. Or shall a serious
> effort be made… to create organs through which the nation can
> control, in co-operation with other nations, its economic desti-
> nies… It is to abolish all advantages and disabilities which have
> their source, not in difference of personal quality, but in dispar-
> ities of wealth, opportunity, social position, and economic
> power. (Tawney, 1953: 60)

Tawney is unequivocal that the creation of a classless society is the
defining attribute of a socialist society, and that those reformists
who stop short of this radical advocacy cannot be regarded as
socialists, whatever their other virtues. Whilst *Equality* embraces
gradualism, in *The Choice Before the Labour Party* Tawney reaffirms
that the ultimate aim is the supersession of capitalism. Having
made clear the revolutionary implications of adhering to the creed,
Tawney turns to the motives of socialists; what is the purpose of the
transformation?

> Naturally, those who accept it may do so for more than one rea-
> son—because they think it more conducive to economic effi-
> ciency than a capitalism which no longer, as in its prime,
> delivers the goods; or merely because they have an eccentric
> prejudice in favour of treating men as men; or, since the reasons
> are not necessarily inconsistent, for both reasons at once. In
> either case, they are socialists. (Tawney, 1953: 60–61)

So although Tawney defines the doctrine with a degree of rigidity,
he is more flexible about the motives of the faithful, accepting that
those who advocate socialism on the basis of efficiency are a legitimate part of the Labour movement. Despite his interpretation of the
Labour Party as the product of class cleavage, Tawney makes the
point that it boasts a more diverse membership than do the other
mainstream parties. Although its cause may be predominantly presented in terms of the advancement of the working class, many of
the professional classes march under its banner, and it is because it
brings together such a diverse group, with differing life experiences, that it needs to find cohesion in a common political creed.
The Party is weakened if individuals are allowed to parade their
idiosyncrasies, regardless of whether they conflict with the purpose
of the Party to create a classless society.

Thus, Tawney's discussion of principles reveals the following
important propositions. First, principles are paramount in a political movement—he emphasizes the importance of 'common intellectual convictions' within the Labour Party (Tawney, 1953: 61).
Failure to adequately define its ideology deprives a party of purpose and knowledge of its long-term objectives and how to attain
them. The events of 1931 were a reflection of this fundamental failing, rather than the personal apostasy of MacDonald. Second, these
principles are of an ethical nature, but this does not require that
they are derived from a transcendental foundation. Tawney reaffirms his abandonment of the position adopted in the *Commonplace
Book*, and to some extent in *The Acquisitive Society*, that moral
improvement is necessarily the product of religiously-inspired ethical ends that are most effectively embodied and propagated by the
Christian Church. Third, principles must be characterized by a
practical dynamic and be capable of application. This reflects
Tawney's long-standing commitment that political concepts are for

use not for ornament. Fourth, the Labour Party has failed to adequately define its brand of socialism, and has abdicated its responsibility to pursue policies that advance the cause of a classless society. This failure will be discussed in the following section when Tawney exposes the consequences of this doctrinal disorder as a programme for government which is a hotchpotch of policies designed to win broad appeal, but which only results in superficial supporters who disperse at the first sign of dispute. Fifth, socialism must be conceived in terms of the creation of a classless society in which individuals are judged on the basis of their personal capacities rather than their socio-economic positions. Finally, both ethical and technocratic brands of the doctrine are valid, reflecting Tawney's growing sympathy for aspects of Fabianism, although the moral appeal of socialism remains the most fundamental basis of his advocacy.

7.2.2 The sectionalism of the Labour Party

Tawney severely criticizes the Labour Party for its internal divisions. As Wright (1987: 102) cogently remarks, Tawney was exasperated by the 'sectarianism of "private socialisms"', and much 'like Orwell, Tawney reserved a particular anger for the dialectical diversions practised by socialist intellectuals in the 1930s'. Tawney's irritation is aroused, for example, by the indiscriminate way in which the Labour Party adopts policies at its party conferences (the sovereign decision-making body of the Party):

> The characteristic vice of the programmes of the party, as set out in conference resolutions, is that too often they are not programmes. They sweep together great things and small; nationalise land, mines and banking in one sentence, and abolish fox-hunting in the next; and, by touching on everything, commit ministers to nothing. (Tawney, 1953: 57)

The lack of an ideological anchorage results in a programme that is an incoherent mixture of the fundamental and the frivolous, more expressive of the sectional claims of the membership than a cohesive programme for change. The broad-based nature of commitments produces a programme that lacks an overriding theme, or a persuasive narrative, blurring the grounds on which a Labour government should be judged, and weakening its paramount goal of economic and social reconstruction. By presenting a policy platform that resembles 'a glittering forest of Christmas trees, with presents for everyone', the Party is demonstrating its inability to prioritize those areas of existence that need to be addressed urgently (Tawney, 1953: 57).

Significantly, in Tawney's view, it is the generalized membership of the Labour Party that is at fault. Just as he is not prepared to attribute the debacle of the Great Betrayal to the machinations of Ramsey MacDonald, he is clear that responsibility for the doctrinal mess must be shared by the movement as a whole and not confined to the upper echelons. The resolutions that form the basis of the Party's programme emerge from the grassroots; they are effectively wish lists reflecting the idiosyncracies of the Party faithful, rather than the reasoned analysis by a membership conscious of the need to form a cohesive programme that is exclusively devoted to the aim of creating a socialist commonwealth. Tawney traces the fault to both the mentality of the membership and the structure of the Party. On the deficiencies of the current membership, although he doesn't go as far as George Orwell in *The Road to Wigan Pier* in dismissing some socialists as cranks—'there is the horrible—the really disquieting—prevalence of cranks wherever Socialists are gathered together. One sometimes gets the impression that the mere words "Socialism" and "Communism" draw towards them with magnetic force every fruit-juice drinker, nudist, sandal-wearer, sex-maniac, Quaker, "Nature Cure" quack, pacifist, and feminist in England' (Orwell, 1989: 161)—Tawney does lament the lack of clarity about fundamental principles among the general membership of the Party.

Tawney also criticizes the structural sectionalism of the Party displayed in the role played by the trade unions. While he held a generally positive opinion of trade unions, particularly during his guild socialist phase when he envisaged their expansion into the realm of economic decision-making, Tawney had long believed that their power within the Party needed to be curbed by limiting their voting rights (Tawney, 1953: 56). *The Choice Before the Labour Party* is permeated by his conviction that the Party is not there to advance the sectional interests of particular elements of the working class, but to seek reform in the broadest sense by the redistribution of power and wealth.

This sectionalism, in both membership and structure, has weakened the Party's electoral appeal. Instead of pitching its message to the nation as a whole as a mass political party should, it gravitates towards particular groups. This failure to reach the whole nation with its project has dangers not only for the Labour Party's electoral success but also for its post-election political success should it succeed in gaining power. Tawney, while commending the capacity of liberal democracies to transform society, is aware that victory through the ballot box will not be the end of opposition. Entrenched economic interests will fight the Labour Party's reform policies all the way:

> The plutocracy consists of agreeable, astute, forcible, self-confident, and, when hard pressed, unscrupulous people, who know pretty well which side their bread is buttered, and intend that the supply of butter shall not run short. (Tawney, 1953: 64)

The Labour Party must, therefore, build up a solid body of ideological support across the country if it is to stand a chance of facing down the counter-revolutionary forces of capitalism:

> In order to prepare for it, it must create in advance a temper and mentality of a kind to carry it through, not one crisis, but a series of crises, to which the Zinovieff letter and the Press campaign of 1931 will prove... to have been mere skirmishes of outposts... If the Labour Party is to tackle its job with some hope of success, it must mobilise behind it a body of conviction as resolute and informed as the opposition in front of it. (Tawney, 1953: 63)

The propagandistic campaigns of the past demonstrate that those with a vested interest in maintaining the capitalist system will resort to tactics that are founded on distortion and executed with a vicious fervour. When the plutocracy is for the first time confronted with a Labour Party not content with tinkering with the system but intent on actively changing it through massive social and economic intervention, their resistance will be relentless. Tawney argued that a Labour government would not be sustained by fair weather friends, or a floating constituency attracted to particular aspects of Labour's programme, but by those willing to embrace socialism and the responsibilities that go with it. Armchair socialists, content to complain about capitalism from the comfort of their living rooms, believing that casting a vote once every five years was sufficient, had to be made aware of the truth that nothing less than a crusade was necessary for fundamental change:

> The Labour Party deceives itself, if it supposes that the mere achievement of a majority will enable it to carry out fundamental measures, unless it has previously created in the country the temper to stand behind it when the great struggle begins... What is needed, is not merely the advocacy of particular measures of Socialist reconstruction, indispensable though that is. It is the creation of a body of men and women who, whether trade unionists or intellectuals, put Socialism first, and whose creed carries conviction, because they live in accordance with it... It is not to encourage adherents to ask what they will get from a Labour Government, as though a campaign were a picnic, all beer and sunshine... It is to make them understand that the return of a Labour Government is merely a struggle the issue of which depends on themselves. (Tawney, 1953: 66)

So victory in the struggle that will follow the election of a Labour government will not only depend on the breadth of its support, but also on the depth of commitment amongst its supporters, who must be prepared for a 'long and arduous struggle' (Tawney, 1953: 58). The crusading role that in the Diaries and in *The Acquisitive Society* Tawney had attributed to the Christian Church is now accorded to the membership of the Labour Party. Whilst his perception of the resources required to forge a new society has not altered, his readiness to situate them in the political realm follows the post-war trajectory of his thought away from the exclusionary Christian stance to a much more secular position. The various alterations that have characterized Tawney's theory since 1914, including acceptance of the capacity of the political realm to generate moral renewal; acknowledgment that morality is not the exclusive preserve of Christians; adoption of a generalized humanism in which concepts such as equal worth are not predicated on a belief in God; displacement of the Church by the Labour Party as the indispensable vehicle of progress; and the centrality of socialism to radical moral, social and political revolution, may tempt us to conclude that the influence of Christianity has diminished to imperceptibility in

Tawney's thought. However, such a judgment would be premature, as his 1937 speech, *A Note on Christianity and the Social Order*, makes clear.

7.3 *A Note on Christianity and the Social Order* (1937)

The writings published after the Diaries show a gradual, but relentless move away from Christian exclusivity—the notion that key concepts are dependent on a belief in God for their authenticity. Our chronological approach has shown that the essentialist thesis that Christianity asserts a continuous formative influence on Tawney's theory is unpersuasive. Whilst it is true that Tawney remained a Christian until his death, the catch-all simplicity of the essentialist interpretation ignores the extent to which Tawney diluted the Christian content of his thought, embracing secular argumentation. Nevertheless, Tawney's subsequent political thought does owe *something* to the religious doctrine, as we saw in *The Acquisitive Society* (1921) and *Religion and the Rise of Capitalism* (1926), and as we can see here in his *A Note on Christianity and the Social Order* (1937), a work which represents his most sustained direct engagement with the role of Christianity in contemporary society. While this speech does not represent a return to the fundamentalism of the Diaries, it does affirm the continuing attraction of Christianity to Tawney as a radical doctrine whose prime value is its counter to the materialism of capitalism.

7.3.1 *Christians and anti-materialism*

Although *A Note on Christianity and the Social Order* is a lecture delivered to a religious conference, Tawney is trying to persuade an organization containing deeply conservative elements to condemn capitalism and embrace an alternative, which while not referred to as socialism in the speech, effectively amounts to the egalitarian doctrine expounded in *Equality*. He is trying to reawaken the social consciousness of the Church to oppose capitalism, not only because capitalism is socially ruinous, but also because it is irreligious. While not reverting back to the position of the Diaries in which religion is prior to politics, *A Note of Christianity and the Social Order* makes use of two arguments to demonstrate the powerful role that religion can play in assisting a radical political agenda. First, the distinctive Christian way of life is diametrically opposed to the materialistic values of market economics. Second, the Christian instinct is egalitarian.

For Tawney, Christianity stood squarely against contemporary materialism:

> Christianity does not merely bear witness against the failures and vices of conventional morality. It repudiates conventional morality's values, objectives and standards of success. (Tawney, 1953: 168)

The capacity for Christian doctrine to legitimize opposition to established norms reflects Tawney's long-held view that, viewed properly, religion is not a conservative force, but one which has revolutionary potential. Tawney's purpose is to persuade an audience of the faithful to embrace Christianity as a social force — i.e. focused not merely on personal conduct, but on the wider political and economic environment. He is providing a pep talk to remind Christians that their vision has massive social implications. However, he has to tread carefully to avoid two landmines. First, he has to emphasize that his message is one of moral, not physical, revolution: while laying down the grounds for a theory of resistance, Tawney is not recommending resistance in any physical sense. Although he talks about the menace of Christianity to the authorities, civil disobedience is not his objective — rather he wants the faithful to concentrate on the social aspect of their Christian doctrine. Second, he must not appear to be too party political: although Tawney is a left-wing partisan within the Church, he is aware of conservative elements that are reluctant to politicize the Church by embracing a political party:

> It is one thing, however, for a church to identify itself with a political party; it is quite another for it to state its own conception of the duties and the rights of men in society, and to determine its attitude to the policies of all parties by the degree to

which they are in agreement with that conception. (Tawney, 1953: 177)

Tawney has to make a case that avoids an overtly political appeal, yet, nevertheless, amounts to a call for social change in a socialistic direction. By avoiding a plea for the Church to align itself with a political organization, but asking it to consider which policies accord with its beliefs, Tawney is preserving the political neutrality of Christianity yet ensuring that religious principles direct members' political engagements. This decision to avoid adopting an overt political position is made by Tawney not only because of the reluctance of the Christian Church to align with a political party, but also because social quietism reigns within the Church that makes it question any social involvement whatsoever. In *Religion and the Rise of Capitalism*, Tawney had lamented the privatization of religion in which it confined itself to matters of personal morality, ignoring the wider social context of immorality. Recognizing the persistence of this tendency within the modern Church, *A Note on Christianity and the Social Order* urges the faithful to examine their social surroundings in terms of their own beliefs:

> Granted, again, that social reconstruction is not a substitute for the Grace of God, it is not self-evident that men prepare themselves best to receive that Grace by deliberately maintaining relations with their fellow-men which they have been expressly warned by Christian thinkers of undisputed authority are both ruinous to their soul and in flagrant contradiction with the teaching of Christ... If Christians limit their liabilities, the devil does not. They may throw him the world of politics and business to devour at his leisure, in the hope that, while gnawing them he will leave such minor morsels as private lives alone. (Tawney, 1953: 175–176)

Christians must not limit their remit to personal conduct, because the economic sphere generates forms of immorality that directly undermine Christian principles. The division between the life of faith and the external order is a false distinction, and Tawney is at pains to highlight those aspects of economic civilization that are an affront to religion (Tawney, 1953: 170–171; 176; 186–187). Mindful of the audience he is addressing, Tawney does not discuss the economic inefficiency of the system; instead he highlights its moral deficiencies: the elevation of material accumulation; the appeal to acquisitive appetites; the subordination of the human being to economics; and the class distinctions that divide the human family. The contrast between capitalism and Christianity's austere code of living is stark:

> 'Give me neither wealth nor poverty, but enough for my sustenance'. Experience suggests that, as those oft-quoted words imply, neither an unceasing struggle against destitution, nor a privileged immunity from the trials of the common lot, offers the environment most conducive to spiritual health. (Tawney, 1953: 189–190)

Indeed, Tawney portrays capitalism as not merely irreligious, but counter-religious (Tawney, 1953: 191). Christians must not take refuge in pious rhetoric, but apply their principles to the world around them:

> The one course which is indefensible is to reiterate platitudes in general terms, while declining, for reasons of prudence, to indicate the direction in which, in the circumstances of today, the attempt to apply Christian principles to society would cause men to move. Such evasions disgust sincere men, and bring Christianity into contempt. (Tawney, 1953: 177)

Tawney's perennial concern with principles as active social forces, therefore, again comes to the fore. He argues that current circumstances provide opportunities for Christians because capitalism is being undermined by moral, intellectual and economic forces, and Tawney expects that in the near future, the ascent of new principles will be confirmed as 'a systematic attempt will be made to apply them' (Tawney, 1953: 189). Tawney is not referring here to a religious revival, but to the election of a Labour government, so he is using religious arguments to foster the success of a secular socialist creed.

It is clear, therefore, that *A Note on Christianity and the Social Order*, while making the important point that religion is still important to Tawney, reflects the change of the balance of power in Tawney's thought. Both the *Commonplace Book* and *The Acquisitive Society* had given a central role to religion in persuading the population to embrace common ends, but this later work, whilst not abandoning the notion that Christians should try and convert the population, is more concerned to convert Christians to a social programme that looks remarkably like socialism. Thus, this religious essay, specifically addressed to the faithful, ironically reveals the extent to which Tawney has supplemented his religious thought with a secular-inclined politics that deprives many of his pre-war religious principles of their centrality.

7.3.2 Christians and egalitarianism

Just as Tawney cleverly turns a traditional Christian belief — anti-materialism — into an argument for socialism, so he turns another traditional Christian belief — equal worth — into another argument for socialism. In *A Note on Christianity and the Social Order*, Tawney suggests that equal worth is an historical inheritance from Christianity which many secular thinkers have embraced; the initial usage of the concept is a religious one, even if those advocating it no longer share the religious underpinning. This argument does not represent a return to the Christian exclusivity of the *Commonplace Book*, because in the Diaries Tawney asserts that the idea has a *conceptual* dependence on the acceptance of the existence of God: only religious thinkers can legitimately lay claim to it. By contrast, in *A Note on Christianity and the Social Order*, Tawney is only concerned to establish the *historical* origin of the notion of equal worth in Christianity. So *A Note on Christianity and the Social Order* demonstrates the historical influence that religion has had on doctrines like equality, without requiring secular thinkers to defer to Christianity to ensure the legitimacy of their advocacy of the concept.

7.4 Conclusion

This chapter has examined two important works that Tawney produced during the 1930s, and found that they throw additional light on his complex journey from Christian exclusivity to secular socialism. In *The Choice Before the Labour Party*, Tawney reiterates his insistence on the primacy of principles in politics, berating the Labour Government for appearing to lose sight of its fundamental *raison d'etre* as a vehicle for socialist values, and for its failure to carry through those values into policy decisions. Mere anunciation of socialist rhetoric was not enough: principles were useless if not put into practice. Tawney criticized the Labour Party's tendency towards sectionalism, both in its tolerance of idiosyncratic or crankish causes, and in its structural bias towards particular interests rather than the national good. In short, the Labour Party seemed to be losing the crusading force which Tawney had invested in it as the surrogate of the Church in promoting a new ethical order.

In *A Note on Christianity and the Social Order*, Tawney revisits the role of Christianity in assisting this moral revolution. In coded language, he affirms that the essence of Christianity is socialism, in that its austere anti-materialism and egalitarianism are prime socialist principles, diametrically opposed to the values of capitalism. Tawney is trying to persuade practising Christians that the political logic of their faith is socialism. This does not mean that he returns to the position he adopted in the Diaries that the political order is subordinated to Christianity — that religion is primary and politics is secondary — but rather that religion is properly seen as supporting a radical critique of the prevailing socio-economic system. As we shall see in the next chapter, in his final years, Tawney somewhat softens the ascetic cast of his anti-materialism, but he does not compromise his commitment to secular principled egalitarianism.

Chapter Eight

Writings from 1938–1952

Revised Editions of Equality (1938 and 1952);
Why Britain Fights (1940);
We Mean Freedom (1944);
Social Democracy in Britain (1949);
and British Socialism Today (1952)

8.1 Introduction

The writings in Tawney's final phase are repetitive, not only in the sense that he re-uses the stock phrases that have served him well over the previous decades, but also because great swathes of passages are replicated from his previous writings. This tendency begins in the late 1930s, prefiguring the general decline detected by Terrill (1973: 106) in Tawney's output during the 1950s: 'Into the 1950s, and his seventies, Tawney began to lose personal mastery. If still active, he was seldom original. He was without the will for fresh initiatives, and not up to the overall rethinking that would justify a big new book on politics.' Terrill's comments are particularly relevant to Tawney as he approaches the 1960s, frequently complaining in his correspondence about his 'diminishing capacity' to do his work and a sense that his intellectual contribution was fading into history. For example, in response to a letter sent by D.F.J. Parsons of the Labour Research Department, Tawney ruefully writes:

> Thank you for comparing me to the Bible. If I resemble it the only likeness is that nobody nowadays believes in either. (Tawney, Tawney/Vyvyan Archive 16, Letter to D.F.J. Parsons, 27th January 1961)

Some tetchiness is also apparent in Tawney's later years, with complaints about the afflictions of old age, and occasional outbursts directed at motorists encroaching on the countryside and farmers using pesticides. For instance, he declares that 'if only the Government would let pedestrians arm themselves, we would settle these brutes, the motorists, in a week', and he appeals to a Miss Gandy, a writer on rural affairs, to 'say something really beastly about the people who sacrifice everything beautiful of that kind to the supposed necessity of cramming more food into people' (Tawney, Tawney/Vyvyan Archive 15, Letter to Miss I Gandy, 3rd February 1961). However, this is the octogenarian Tawney; the writings of the late forties and early fifties do not indicate such eccentricity. Although he is performing an intellectual stocktaking before closing down his contribution to the socialist project, these essays do improve our understanding of Tawney's intellectual trajectory, with important discussions of democracy, liberty, and the achievements and failures of socialism. This final chapter will concentrate on the revised editions of *Equality* in 1938 and 1952, and the essays *Why Britain Fights* (1940); *We Mean Freedom* (1944); *Social Democracy in Britain* (1949); and *British Socialism Today* (1952). The other writings of this period, including Tawney's unremarkable study of the American Labour Movement (1942; see Tawney, 1979), and his book on the career of the merchant Lionel Cranfield, *Business & Politics Under James I* (1958) — about which Tawney confesses to being 'ashamed to have devoted so much time to it', and says that he should have 'turned my hand to something more useful and readable' (Tawney, Tawney/Vyvyan Archive 16, Letter to Father Larkin, 17th February 1961) — are not relevant to our concerns.

8.2 Revised edition of *Equality* (1938)

The 1938 edition of *Equality*, with its new concluding chapter that reflected Tawney's increasing concern with the democratic credentials of the Labour Party, is a significant clarification of Tawney's views on the nature of democracy, giving credence to Wootton's (1952: 261) comments that the differing versions of *Equality* reveal the evolution of Tawney's political thought. The rise of Hitler, combined with the impending threat of international conflict and the news emerging from the Soviet Union about the liquidation of the peasantry, brought into sharp focus the need to defend democratic norms. In addition, Tawney's conviction that the Labour Party and socialism, rather than the Church and Christianity, were the main instruments of social, moral and political progress, framed his discussion. In this revised edition, Tawney borrows chunks of passages from *The Choice Before the Labour Party* (Tawney, 1938: 274–275; 277) to reiterate his call for the creation of a temper for change in the country, and an acceptance that peaceful parliamentary reform is the optimal route to socialism. But an additional element is a more enriched concept of democracy, which embraces the notion that democracy is more than merely a method of government, but also a way of life.

The reason for Tawney's extended discussion of democracy is his perception that it is under threat, not merely in countries with chequered histories where democratic procedures have always been fragile, but also in Britain, despite its long history of constitutional government. Britain faces challenges both from the left, attracted by the allure of nostrums of 'real' democracy embodied in the idea of the Soviet, and from the right: in 1934 Tawney played a major role in a Labour Party discussion group which, responding to the political abuses that occurred in Germany, looked at the possibility that right-wing elements in Britain would attempt to sabotage a democratically-elected Labour government (Durbin, 1985: 189).

In this analysis of the threats from both the right and the left to democracy in Britain, Tawney employs the argument that Britain's professed commitment to freedom is a mirage, since the virtues of liberty are professed, but not followed, because a substantial section of the population are denied full citizenship by economic circumstances (Tawney, 1938: 249–251). Freedom is only meaningful when it is connected with practical powers that allow individuals to exercise their capacities; continued social and economic inequalities impede progress towards democracy. Although this reflection leads Tawney to question whether democracy can survive in Britain, he does not regurgitate the discourse of collapse that features in *The Acquisitive Society*; indeed he dismisses the alarmist talk that Britain will succumb to a 'gentlemanly Fascism', as 'panic not politics' (Tawney, 1938: 259). He does stress, however, that democracy will remain insecure if it continues to be confined to the political sphere: it must be embraced as a way of life by society as a whole. This argument is developed by means of an analysis of the meaning of democracy in terms of three cornerstones — consent, accountability and common humanity:

> authority, to justify its title, must rest on consent; that power is tolerable only so far as it is accountable to the public; and that differences of character and capacity between human beings, however important on their own plane, are of minor significances compared with the capital fact of their common humanity. Its object is to extend the application of those principles from the sphere of civil and political rights, where, at present, they are nominally recognised, to that of economic and social organisation, where they are systematically and insolently defied. The socialist movement and the Labour party exist for that purpose. (Tawney, 1938: 260)

These assertions indicate that Tawney sees democracy not merely as a method of government, but as a type of society: it is not only a mechanism to deliver power, but a substantive moral principle in itself that defines a civilized community. Moreover, Tawney stresses that democracy is the first premise of socialism, and that 'all nods, winks and other innuendos' that violence is an option are 'ruled out for good and all', and that once the democratic line is accepted, 'socialists must adhere to it, when it is not to their advantage as well as when it is' (Tawney, 1938: 268).

In any case, liberal democracy in Britain is not an option for socialists, but a fact of political life, bequeathed by centuries of constitutional development:

Unlike that of central Europe, and still more that of Russia, it
has been steeped for two centuries in a liberal tradition, and the
collapse of political Liberalism has not effaced the imprint. The
result is the existence of a body of opinion, larger, probably,
than in most other countries, which is sensitive on such subjects
as personal liberty, freedom of speech and meeting, tolerance,
the exclusion of violence from politics, parliamentary government — what, broadly, it regards as fair play and guarantees for
it. The only version of socialism which, as things are to-day, has
the smallest chance of winning mass support, is one which
accepts that position. (Tawney, 1938: 266)

The working class's adherence to the liberal inheritance 'whether
admirable or regrettable... remains a fact' (Tawney, 1938: 267) — i.e.
it is ingrained in the national psyche of the populace. Tawney
stresses that socialism must accept this historical legacy of liberal
democracy, wearing a 'local garb' to appeal to the 'mental and
moral traditions of plain men and women', using its ideology to
persuade, not browbeat (Tawney, 1938: 265; 266). A realistic socialist strategy must acknowledge that the masses would always
favour a democratic capitalism over an undemocratic socialism. In
a more positive vein, Tawney urges the Labour Party to see this
democratic inheritance as a source of 'latent energy' to be called
upon to support its cause:

Democracy ought not to be regarded merely as political mechanism — a mechanism which, indeed, it is important to preserve,
but which in the absence of a Fascist revolution, can be taken for
granted. It ought to be envisaged as a force to be released. The
Labour Party, in particular, should think of it, not merely in
terms of ballot-boxes, and majorities, but as a vast reservoir of
latent energies — a body of men and women who, when inert,
are a clog, but may become, once stirred into action, a dynamic
incalculable power. Its function is not merely to win votes; it is
to wake the sleeping demon. It is to arouse democracy to a sense
both of the possibilities within its reach, and of the dangers
which menace it; to put it on its mettle; to make it militant and
formidable. (Tawney, 1938: 276)

However, Wright draws a parallel between these statements by
Tawney and Leninism, a tradition far removed from the peaceful
realms of parliamentary democracy: 'There is even a whiff of Leninism, a version of "consciousness from without", in this account of

how the masses who are typically "inert" and "a clog" have to be energised by a "New Model" army of dedicated socialists' (Wright, 1987: 120). Although a more appropriate analogy to Tawney's insistence on the capacity of the masses to forge the new society from within the Marxian tradition might be drawn with either Karl Kautsky or Rosa Luxemburg, there does seem to be a disjunction between Tawney's belief in a peaceful transition to socialism through the existing mechanism of political power, and his expression of the dynamism of the masses, which seems more suited to a theory of revolutionary overthrow. At any rate, Tawney fails to explain how this 'vast reservoir of latent energies' would manifest itself in a parliamentary democracy.

At the conclusion of the 1938 edition of *Equality*, Tawney reaffirms the belief he expressed in *The Choice Before the Labour Party* that the Labour Party should not be an organization of one particular class, nor should it be reduced to the political wing of the trade union movement. It must have a more expansive appeal capable of attracting a diverse range of individuals to its cause:

> It is not a question, of course, of giving second place to the claims of industrial workers, who are capitalism's chief victims, but of presenting those claims as what in essence they are, a demand for a life that is worthy of human beings, and which no decent man will withhold from his fellows. The appeal to them, in short, must be based upon principles, which unite men who in their interest and experience may be poles asunder. (Tawney, 1938: 279–280)

Having responded to the approach of conflict by defending democracy during the war, Tawney turns to the arrangements that should prevail after the Fascist foe had been defeated. Much like the conflagration of 1914–18, the Second World War stimulated changes in Tawney's theory, especially in his concept of liberty.

8.3 *Why Britain Fights* (1940);
We Mean Freedom (1944)

The First World War was a catalyst for Tawney's thought, leading him to accept the need for institutional mechanisms to advance the progressive cause. Beyond this, he argued that the conflict irrevocably altered the mentality of the British public, creating the expectation that radical reforms would be initiated to set the country on a more egalitarian course. The conflagration of 1939–45 had a less profound influence, although Tawney, in his stirring essay, *Why Britain Fights* (1940), again presents the conflict as a defence of the British way of life: 'We can lay no claim to any special virtue, for though we dislike fighting, we dislike it less than the alternative. We prefer dying on our feet to living on our knees' (Tawney, 1953: 75–76). On the content of the British way of life, Tawney has this to say:

> The nature and quality of that way of life can be stated in a dozen different fashions… Good faith; tolerance; respect for opinions which we do not share; loyalty to comrades; mercy to the weak; consideration for the unfortunate; equal justice for all… the power to speak freely one's own thoughts, to obey one's own conscience, to do one's duty as one sees it. So is the right of the individual to be protected against violence, whether proceeding from other individuals or from public authorities; to live under a Government which he has a voice in making and unmaking; to work by all lawful means to promote the reforms and advance the causes which command his devotion, however repugnant they may be to his rulers. (Tawney, 1953: 73)

Although Tawney had always lauded the historic freedoms of Britain, hitherto he had not done so in terms of the doctrine of abstract rights (though he did enunciate a notion of natural rights in *The New Leviathan*), preferring to emphasize the subordination of rights to obligations, seeing individuals as instruments of social purposes. But the thirties and forties saw a greater emphasis by him on the language of rights and the importance of individual liberties. The later essays, composed not merely in a period of European authoritarianism, but in which there was widespread material deprivation, intensified Tawney's discussion of freedom, diluting the austere and duty-based conceptions of the early writings, to embrace a more easy-going approach, with the accent on 'essential liberties'.

The 1944 essay, *We Mean Freedom*, is Tawney's most concentrated and effective discussion of liberty. He begins from the proposition that everyone in Britain values freedom:

> My subject is 'We Mean Freedom.' No doubt, we do; but then so, in his opinion, at least in this country, does everyone else, including the House of Lords, the Conservative Party, the Press, the Stock Exchange, and a miscellaneous assortment of bankers, industrialists, and landowners, all of whom cry aloud and cut themselves with knives at the thought that the liberties of the country may be menaced. (Tawney, 1953: 82–83)

The problem is that everyone in Britain does not mean the same thing by the term 'freedom'. Whilst Tawney is typically not interested in a conceptual analysis of the term, he is fully aware of its ambivalence, and his purpose is to demonstrate that the socialist notion of effective freedom is the most plausible interpretation. Defying the simplistic judgment that liberals prize liberty while socialists privilege equality, Tawney elucidates his notion of effective freedom to demonstrate that liberty is meaningless as a practical doctrine without the existence of accessible choices. In asserting the superiority of the socialist conception of freedom, Tawney couches his discussion in terms of essential rights, thereby diluting, but not abandoning, his commitment to duties. This reorientation of his thought is evident in three respects: the crafting of a concept of liberty that avoids the austerity of his previous works; the embracing of a doctrine of primary liberties that alters his earlier adherence to common ends; and the welcoming of state intervention that modifies his liberal commitment to economic experimentation. The first and second of these reorientations is evident in *We Mean Freedom*; the second and third are evident in *Social Democracy in Britain*, *British Socialism Today*, and in the 1952 edition of *Equality*.

The concept of freedom that Tawney expressed in early works such as the *Commonplace Book* and *The Acquisitive Society* is characterized by an austere outlook, strictly subordinating rights to duties. But in *We Mean Freedom* (1944), he formulates a definition of liberty that puts more emphasis on self-development than on duties:

It is free in so far, and only so far, as all the elements composing
it are able in fact, not merely in theory, to make the most of their
powers to grow to their full stature, to do what they conceive to
be their duty, but — since liberty should not be too austere — to
have their fling when they feel like it. (Tawney, 1953: 84)

This is not an apology for hedonism or a denial of the superiority of
higher ends, but a concession that the contemporary equivalents of
pushpin are part of liberty if the individual chooses them, and citizens should not be entirely subsumed by the pursuit of an edifying
existence. The key to liberty is to allow individuals to fulfil 'what
they [themselves] conceive to be their duty' (Tawney, 1953: 84).
Tawney is not prescriptive in outlining a set of obligations which
the citizen is required to meet; rather individuals are given scope to
determine their own responsibility. But this is not sanctioning
licence in which individuals are free to do as they see fit regardless
of the social consequences: Tawney's views on education show that
he saw it as a means of allowing individuals to make their own
intelligent choices. Nevertheless, he comes close to endorsing the
substance of a notion of a natural right to liberty, even though he
shies away from using that terminology:

Every individual possesses certain requirements — ranging
from material necessities of existence to express himself in
speech and writing to share and worship God in his own way or
to refrain from worshipping Him — the satisfaction of which is
necessary to his welfare... it is not my intention to add yet
another catalogue of essential rights to liberties of such lists that
already exist. (Tawney, 1953: 83)

8.4 *Social Democracy in Britain* (1949); *British Social-ism Today* (1952); and the 1952 edition of *Equality*

The notion of basic 'requirements' is not a departure from Tawney's
earlier thinking, as it is contained in his notion of common humanity, but its linkage with essential rights is a change. Although there
is potential congruence between humans possessing fundamental

needs and a body of rights that relates to their fulfilment, Tawney, in the early works (other than in the abandoned *The New Leviathan*), does not propose a connection. Even in the first edition of *Equality*, which concentrates on the requirement to meet fundamental human needs, he does not couch the argument in terms of essential rights. But given his preparedness to use the term 'essential rights' in *We Mean Freedom*, the question arises: Is Tawney now embracing the doctrine of abstract rights? The answer to this question is certainly not abstract in the sense of having no concrete shape or grounding in practical reality—Tawney's effective freedom demands only rights that can practicably be exercised by all—but yes, abstract in the sense that there is a body of rights that is not entirely dependent on the common good. Tawney adopts this interpretation of freedom also in the 1949 essay, *Social Democracy in Britain*, which replicates much of the 1944 piece, while the epilogue contained in the final edition of *Equality* (1952) goes further still in expressing his conversion to the doctrine of core rights, making a distinction between 'primary' and 'secondary' liberties:

> Liberty is composed of liberties. Certain liberties may be described as primary, essential or fundamental in the sense that, in free societies, they are normally secured by law to all citizens; that they are regarded, not merely as matters of convenience, but as principles on which the State is based; and that, when written constitutions exist, they are often included in them. Other liberties are narrower in their range and less crucial in their content. They are in their nature, less of principles, then expedients or 'devices' to be extended or restricted in the light of changing circumstances, and may, properly, for that reason, be classed as secondary. (Tawney, 1964a: 227)

Primary liberties are those fundamental entitlements like freedom of movement, speech and assembly which are a *sine qua non* of modern democracy. Secondary liberties are not given a philosophically- satisfactory definition, but drawing on the work of the architect of the welfare state, William Beveridge, Tawney intimates that they are connected with economic activity, such as the ownership of productive property and the expenditure of income (Tawney, 1964a: 228; 245). The purpose of the distinction is to confront the argument that egalitarianism necessarily entails the loss of core freedoms;

Tawney argues that socialist measures operate within the realms of secondary rights, and rather than impeding primary rights, enhance them, by enabling individuals to exercise their entitlements, thereby producing an enriched liberty:

> It will reflect, in the first place, that, if the rights essential to freedom are effectively to safeguard it, they must not be merely formal, like the right of all who can afford it to dine at the Ritz, but must be accompanied by conditions which ensure that, when ever the occasion to exercise them arises, they can in fact be exercised... Measures which, by diminishing inequality, have helped convert these nominal rights into practical powers, have made, in the strictest sense, a contribution to freedom. They have turned it from an iridescent abstraction into a sober reality of everyday life. (Tawney, 1964a: 234–235)

Whilst Tawney here does not directly confirm that he proposes a body of rights which are free from spatial and temporal considerations, his acceptance that free societies are normally based on the attainment and maintenance of these fundamental or primary rights or liberties, which are to be contrasted with secondary rights because they are principles not expedients or devices to be 'extended or restricted in light of changing circumstances', suggests a body of inalienable rights, which government should be bound by and seek to enhance. Even if there is doubt that this is a conversion to natural rights, it is undeniable that Tawney's attitude to rights has significantly altered from the early works. The ideas of *The Acquisitive Society* would not allow Tawney to make the primary/ secondary split, because, although he would be able to discriminate between the degrees of importance of different liberties, they would all be in the secondary category, legitimately withdrawn when they conflicted with the common good. As the quotations above show, Tawney now argues that the state is based on rights that are in the primary category, and therefore key aspects of society are now subordinate to rights, rather than liberties being entirely subsumed by duties, as in the early Tawney.

There is, therefore, a gap between the early and later Tawney, in which the balance between freedom and duties has shifted, altering the character of his thought. Although Tawney always valued individual empowerment as a condition of a healthy society, in his early writings there is a tendency for his assertion of duties and his asceticism to imbue agents with passivity, and to restrict choices to those that will nourish spiritual and intellectual development. His concept of freedom was then saturated with austerity, or, as critics like Greenleaf claim, a meanness, that deprives it of human warmth and shackles the agent to high-minded duties. Chambers (1971: 365), dealing primarily with Tawney the historian, commented that the later Tawney was marked by an 'incipient form of mellowing, or a blunting of the sharp edge of dogmatic certainty'. This shift is particularly telling in relation to Tawney's later discussion of liberty and rights. His comment that individuals should have their fling when they feel like it is not a throwaway remark but represents a re-orientation of his idea of liberty. He is building in a conception of frivolous fun for individuals who were previously enveloped by duties as instruments of social purpose, and whose freedom was solely concentrated on the pursuit of edifying activities.

> What matters most is the kind of life people lead and the satisfaction they find in it. And here, I suspect, most of us are apt to think too much of problems and too little of persons; too much in terms of evils to be cured, and too little of happiness to be increased. (Tawney, 1964b)

In *British Socialism Today*, happiness, which Tawney had in *The Acquisitive Society* disparaged as an individualistic or even selfish value that undermined the unity of common ends, becomes an important element of a socialist political platform which Tawney urges his readers to acknowledge and value. Duty remains an integral part of Tawney's thought, but it is less of a lofty imposition with individuals performing their duties than an opportunity for creativity, with individuals being empowered to find their own way, within reasonable boundaries. Finally, he dilutes his conception of duties to ensure that rights are not merely an appendage of obligations, but have an independent existence, with key institutions revolving around their maintenance and extension.

However, there is one sphere of social life about which the mature Tawney became less, rather than more, libertarian — the sphere of the economy. Tawney has traditionally been depicted as an advocate of economic experimentation in which different modes of ownership, including private, can continue to operate, provided that they meet social purposes. For example, Freeden (1986: 316), drawing primarily on *The Acquisitive Society*, argues that Tawney's flexibility in relation to the forms of ownership and organization showed 'a close affinity to liberal experimentation'. However, while this may be true of the views that Tawney expressed in 1921 in *The Acquisitive Society*, if we examine his economic prescriptions in the 1940s and 1950s it is apparent that his liberal acceptance of experimentation is a good deal more circumscribed.

Before examining these later views, it is worth noting that even in *The Acquisitive Society*, Tawney imposes limits on liberal economic experimentation. First, an interpretation of the notion of Social Function (the key principle in *The Acquisitive Society*) as tolerating private modes of ownership providing they meet social ends, neglects the fact that Social Function is premised not merely on the attainment of common ends, but on the intentions and motives of the agent (Tawney, 1921: 9). Tawney does not merely want private property to deliver social benefits, but he also demands that the owner's intentions are animated by the principle of social service. Thus, Function has a deontological feature that sets a much stiffer test than whether the enterprise in question generates social benefits. The motivation of agents is important in Tawney's advocacy of Functional property, because otherwise it could collapse into a Smithian invisible hand argument in which social benefits are the unintended affects of self-regarding actions, with acquisitive appetites being endorsed if they produced benign social consequences. This requirement that the agent's intentions need to be morally benign, demonstrates that for Tawney, there are ethical limits on the kind of economic experimentation that is legitimate. Second, Tawney's commitment to economic experimentation is restricted by the Fabian ideas that he put forward in *The Acquisitive Society*, including advocating the nationalization of the commanding heights of the economy, such as coal, banks, transport, power and steel, and emphasizing that private concerns should operate in a framework established by a national authority, with the state possessing sufficient power to ensure the public interest.

In the 1940s, however, these limitations on economic experimentation become concrete and explicit. For example, in *We Mean Free-*

dom, although he rejects the idea of state intervention in every aspect of the economy, he insists that the government must have control over the major economic enterprises:

> it is not necessary that a single central body should intervene in every corner of economic life; it is enough that the sector controlled by it should be sufficiently important to enable the State to take or determine the major decisions on matters such as investment, credit policy and employment, on which general welfare depends. It is not necessary that it should plan every detail of production; it is sufficient that it should issue to the public utility corporations... instructions as to the general policy which they are to pursue... with regard to output, costs, prices and erection of new plants. (Tawney, 1953: 96–97)

Although Tawney considers these proposals modest, they helped to fuel anxieties held by classical liberals such as Hayek (whose influential *The Road to Serfdom* was published in 1944) about the totalitarian tendencies of state intervention (Hayek, 1944). Tawney responded to this anxiety in his later essays, defending the efficacy of state action in general; distinguishing British socialism from its Soviet counterpart and supporting the reforms of the Attlee Administration, whilst acknowledging their limitations. For example, in *Social Democracy in Britain*, Tawney attacks the philosophical tradition that views the state as an entity in itself, with its own ends. Combining his distrust of abstract speculation with his conviction that the 'only sound test of a political system, is its effects on the lives of human beings', Tawney rejects the Hegelian, Marxist and Freudian conceptions of the State (Tawney, 1964b: 141; 164). Typically, rather than confront these theories on their own level with a philosophical dissection, Tawney simply dismisses them as irrational:

> The idea that there is an entity called 'the State', which possesses, in virtue of its title, uniform characteristics, existing independently of the varying histories, economic environments, constitutional arrangements, legal systems and social psychologies of particular states... is a pure superstition. (Tawney, 1964b: 164)

For Tawney, state structures display the imprint of the society in which they develop, and rather than function according to some internal dynamic, the state is merely an instrument subordinate to the demands of its social setting. Accordingly, Tawney (1964b: 163) rejects the argument of *The Road to Serfdom*, arguing that the expansion of the state in England demonstrates that Hayek's 'bloodthirsty Leviathan becomes a serviceable drudge'. Tawney points out that the democratic credentials of the post-war expansion of the British state undermine any comparisons between British Social Democracy and Communism, and expose the alarmism of Hayek, who is caricatured by Tawney (1964b: 165) as the 'nervous professor' wedded to 'high theory'. Whilst acknowledging the economic achievements of the Soviet Government, Tawney stresses that this is no substitute for human rights, and that the 'contrast between Russian Police Collectivism and the socialism of Western Europe is too obvious to need emphasis' (Tawney, 1964b: 158). Planning, far from representing a creeping totalitarianism, has been conducted in Britain under democratic scrutiny, and this has led to the extension of liberty, not its diminution, because it is a rational response to the demands of a political democracy with the needs of the people driving the agenda. Half-hearted attempts at economic reform have failed in Britain: Tawney (1964b: 162) draws a distinction between previous and recent remodelling of the state — past governments introduced reforms 'hesitatingly and with reluctance', whereas the Attlee administration is driving through reforms 'rapidly and with conviction'.

Tawney's assessment of the Labour Government 1945–51 is, therefore, positive, but it is also qualified. On the positive side, the *dirigiste* views of the mature Tawney leads him to take pride in the achievements of the Attlee Government. Over a wide field of its activities, from the redistribution of wealth to the nationalization of core industries, the provision of communal services, and the reduction of poverty Tawney trumpets progress (Tawney, 1964a: 145–154; 171–180; 211–224). As well as extolling the effectiveness of particular policies, Tawney also highlights a more general achievement of the Labour Government:

> It showed that a capitalist economy is not the solid, monolithic block, to be endured as a whole, or overthrown as a whole, that some simpletons suggested. It proved that a Socialist Government, with the public behind it, can change the power relations of the system, can ensure that a large part of the resources yielded by it are devoted to raising the standard of life of the

mass of the population, and can compel those directing it to
work on lines which, left to themselves, they would not choose.
(Tawney, 1964b: 172)

The gradualist tint of Tawney's post-*Acquisitive Society* writings is
evident here, as is a glimmer of the revisionism that will be developed by Crosland in the mid-1950s to dilute the austere strains of
the socialism exemplified by the early Tawney. The Attlee reforms,
backed by an overwhelming democratic mandate from the people,
have made significant inroads, yet with aspects of socialism
co-existing with capitalism. This is not so much an accommodation
with capitalism as an acknowledgment that parliamentary democracy limits the speed of reform, and entails frequent shifts of power
between left and right, so that it is to be expected that the Attlee
reforms will be altered by Conservative governments. The fact that
Tawney's (1964b: 172) embrace of gradualism has not dented his
radicalism is confirmed when he charges future Labour governments with the task of removing 'successive segments of industrial
life from direction by profit-making entrepreneurs', and cautions
against complacency, stressing that the further development of
social democracy is not inevitable, but will require considerable resolution — 'in the absence of sustained and strenuous efforts the way
is as likely to lead down hill as up, and that Socialism, if achieved,
will be the creation, not of any mystical historical necessity, but of
the energy of human minds and wills' (Tawney, 1964b: 170).

On the negative side, Tawney regrets that the Attlee Government
has made little attempt to stimulate a psychological shift, whereby
workers no longer regard themselves as instruments for ends
imposed from above, but play an active part in the management of
the economic enterprises. Although Tawney does not resort to the
guild socialism of *The Acquisitive Society*, he does express disap-
pointment in the participative record of the state-run sector,
lamenting that the nationalized industries have adopted a traditional hierarchical structure, failing to encourage the foundation of
an economic democracy in which power and responsibility is
devolved to the workers. Tawney (1964b: 174; 176) warns of the
threat of excessive bureaucracy and remote management, with the
failure of parliament to impose an effective supervisory regime on
the nationalized industries. Moreover, while the material condi-

tions of the worker have undoubtedly improved, and Labour has made great strides in civilizing society, that vital leap to a socialist society in which quality rules over quantity, public well-being trumps private opulence, and the satisfaction of common humanity is the guiding light, has proved elusive.

> Civilisation is a matter, not of quantity of possessions, but quality of life. It is to be judged, not by the output of goods and services, but by the use made of them. A society which values public welfare above private display; which, though relatively poor, makes the first charge on its small resources the establishment for all of the conditions of a vigorous and self-respecting existence; which gives a high place among those conditions to the activities of the spirit and the services which promote them; which holds the most important aspects of human beings is not external differences of income and circumstances that divide them, but the common humanity that unites them, and which strives, therefore, to reduce such differences to a position of insignificance that rightly belongs to them — such a society may be far from what it should be, but it has, at least, set its face towards the light. It is such a society which British socialists are labouring to create. (Tawney, 1964b: 167)

8.5 Conclusion

In this chapter on the final phase of Tawney's work, although the power and quality of his writings have deteriorated, he still adds some new contributions to his political theory. The most important of these contributions are to his understanding of the concepts of democracy, liberty, and socialism. On democracy, Tawney argues that it will only be secure politically when it is secure socially and economically — i.e. when it has become a way of life for the population, ingrained in their DNA. Moreover, when that occurs, socialists must accept the need to work within democracy, rather than attempt to achieve left-wing objectives by non-parliamentary means. On liberty, Tawney further dilutes the austere, duty-laden conception of his early writings by embracing the more liberal notion of individuals choosing their own personal path to self-development, though in the economic sphere, he argues for government intervention to ensure that the public good is promoted. Accordingly, Tawney applauds the Attlee Government for significantly moving towards socialism by its nationalization initiatives, although he cautions that these huge bureaucracies will have to be monitored to ensure that they remain accountable.

However, his lifelong aversion to materialism impels Tawney to remind readers that socialism is not solely about the growth and equitable distribution of prosperity, but also about the improvement in the quality of life. Notwithstanding his praise for the Attlee administration, therefore, Tawney is fearful that social democracy could make significant *material* difference without achieving a qualitative shift to a more *morally edifying* society. Indeed, towards the end of his life, Tawney declares that socialism had been dehumanized; a bitter lament from a theorist who had spent much of his life championing socialism as the antidote to the institutionalized materialism of capitalism. In one respect, therefore, Tawney has come full circle, returning to the musings of the Diaries with his concern that mainstream socialism, particularly Fabianism, may tidy the room, but might not open a window in the soul. Ironically, the thinker who returned to this theme had himself undergone considerable change, which whilst not surrendering to materialism, did make considerable concessions to the secular age. Far from his work reflecting the 'massive' consistency that orthodox interpretations suggest, Tawney's views on politics are full of paradox.

Chapter Nine

Conclusion

9.1 Introduction

In response to the death of Beatrice Webb in 1943, Tawney wrote a valedictory essay for the British Academy, praising the dedication and tenacity with which she, and her husband Sidney, pursued their intellectual projects. In this essay, Tawney makes the point that, like 'those of most writers who have been active over a long period, the books of the Webbs reflect different phases in their author's lives and thoughts' (Tawney, 1953: 107). Ironically, Tawney himself has been denied a similar treatment by commentators who hold that his work is characterized by an overwhelming unity and consistency, viewing his project as undergoing only minor changes that do not invalidate this essentialist analysis of his thought, and who see nothing amiss in imbuing the private pre-war Diaries with major interpretative significance in understanding Tawney's thought as a whole. Terrill's essentialist analysis is, despite its eclecticism, the most boldly conceptual, with his assumption of a systematic Tawney, focussing on his core concepts as integral entities. Wright informs the reader that Tawney's work displays a 'massive unity, consistency and coherence', and although he accepts that it is difficult to deduce the extent of the religious influence on the published works, the posthumous publication of the pre-war Diaries ends the doubts, demonstrating that Christianity is the 'unstated core' of Tawney's sanctioned intellectual output. So the early private musings of Tawney that were not intended for publication are the platform for understanding the fundamental basis of Tawney's published thought. Although Greenleaf is less enamoured of the Diaries, he argues likewise that the works which Tawney selected for publication exhibit the 'continuous formative influence' of Christian moralism, and he asserts that *The Acquisitive Society* and *Equality* are essentially thorough exemplifications of the themes of the *Commonplace Book*.

Whilst we do not deny that there is a thematic persistence in Tawney's thought, in that the mature Tawney continues to address the issues that engaged him as a young man, we do not accept that his treatment of these themes remained uniform through a period of considerable personal and political change. Applying Skinner's critique of the 'myth of coherence', we argue that these essentialist interpretations of Tawney's political theory fall into the trap of imposing an artificial unity on a body of writing that shifted significantly in its emphasis during the period of nearly 40 years in which it was composed. We claim that a chronological approach to Tawney's writings provides a more authentic representation of his thought. It enables us to demonstrate that Tawney's thought is, contrary to the orthodoxy, not entirely consistent, but characterized by considerable change, particularly, but not exclusively evident in the movement from a Christian exclusivity in which he held certain concepts to be dependent on God, to a position which admitted and often emphasized the validity of secular interpretations of political values. In this concluding chapter, we summarize our findings, not by reiterating the conclusions of the earlier chapters, which have concentrated on Tawney texts, but by extracting from them his interpretations of six major concepts in his political thought, and showing how, contrary to the essentialist interpretation, Tawney's treatment of the first two concepts — ethics and democracy — is fundamentally inconsistent; and how, contrary to the essentialist interpretation, Tawney's treatment of the other four concepts — religion, politics, equality and liberty — altered fundamentally over the course of time. Finally, we show the significance of the findings of this chronological approach for Tawney scholarship, and how it might, if accepted, impact on future studies of Tawney.

9.2 Ethics

In the case of the concepts of ethics and democracy, our argument against the essentialist interpretation is that it fails to acknowledge how inconsistent Tawney is in his analysis of them. By searching for an underlying unity in Tawney's political theory, essentialist commentators tend to gloss over inconvenient inconsistencies and confusions in Tawney's arguments. The chronological approach, which does not seek to impose an artificial coherence where none exists, does not disguise the illogicalities in Tawney's work. Illogicality is particularly evident is Tawney's treatment of ethics.

Despite Tawney's deserved reputation as the leading proponent of ethical socialism, his early moral stance was characterized by a confusion that the subsequent works did not dispel. We argue that the Diaries do not provide a systematic discussion of ethics because Tawney articulates distinct views that do not strictly cohere. For instance, he argues in the Diaries that Christianity possesses a monopoly of morality, with right and wrong dependent on a transcendental, mystical doctrine. He claims that this knowledge resides in each of us, implying that, like his non-rational advocacy of God's existence, it is a product of mystical intuition. However, Tawney also states that moral knowledge is derived from the social harmony that has resulted from the observance of Christian precepts. So, the validity of Christian prescriptions derives from two independent sources: first, their inherent or intuitive 'rightness' — when Christian principles are stated, no-one would venture to deny them. Second, their 'utilitarian' value — the social consequences of not following them are very harmful. But these two sources could generate contradictory moral prescriptions. For example, social harmony was claimed by some Christians in the eighteenth century to be maintained by the institution of slavery — a claim that contradicts Christian moral intuitions. This lack of clarity was present at the inception of Tawney's thought and persisted until the end. To a large extent, the confusion arises from the nature of Tawney's theorizing, in his unwillingness to deal with issues in an abstract or systematic manner. Our chronological interpretation, unlike the essentialist interpretation, does not set out to resolve such inconsistencies, but to authentically represent the confusing nature of aspects of Tawney's thought.

9.3 Democracy

The second concept on which Tawney is inconsistent is democracy. Tawney is often presented as offering a fundamentally democratic conception of socialism, reflected in his faith in parliamentary democracy, and his rejection of the Soviet Union's model of democratic centralism (state socialism). But our chronological interpretation demonstrates that Tawney's commitment to democracy is less clear-cut and more confusing than orthodox interpretations allow. We can see this in his discussion of guilds in *The Acquisitive Society*, which avoids any extensive analysis of the impact of the new guilds on traditional British democratic institutions. When this is considered alongside Tawney's celebration of the virtues of individual subordination to the collective, and his perception that the descent into barbarism can only be averted by embracing the Functional Society, whose democratic credentials are questionable, it is not fanciful to detect an authoritarian streak or, at the very least, a democratic deficit in Tawney's theory.

Moreover, the view formulated by Terrill and Halsey and Dennis that Tawney saw democracy as more than a political system, but as a way of life, is problematic. Certainly in various speeches, Tawney did identify a more elevated conception of democracy, and passages in *Equality* have a Luxemburgian tone, with his appeal for the masses not to be dismissed as voting fodder, but to be utilized as a reservoir of energy. However, these rhetorical flourishes, which seem more pertinent to revolutionary upheaval than to legislative reform, contrast with Tawney's espousal of constitutionalism. The confusion is compounded by Tawney's description of democracy as a tool to be judged by its results, which hardly reflects the more enriched conception that he was also proposing. Equally, in his argument that the Labour Party should commit itself to democracy, Tawney oscillates between an instrumental and a principled defence. In *Equality*, he urges the Labour Party to embrace parlia-mentarianism more as a strategic expedient rather than as a funda-mental principle derived from common humanity. He impresses on the Party that because the British people are saturated with liberal values, and that any party which fails to acknowledge this will fail at the ballot box, it was in the Labour Party's electoral interests to advocate democracy, and once they were committed to it, they must do permanently. There is a paradox here: the Labour Party should endorse democracy for pragmatic reasons, but then adhere to democracy as if it were a principle that should never be surrendered.

These ambivalences indicate that generalized judgments that identify Tawney, in Hugh Gaitskell's words, as 'the democratic socialist, par excellence' (Gaitskell quoted in Tawney, 1964b: 7), are too simplistic. The truth is that Tawney's discussion is question-begging, lacking the clarity that is demanded by conceptual approaches such as the essentialist interpretation. By avoiding such interpretations, there is no temptation to force coherence by identi-fying an essentialist Tawney position. By allowing the contradic-tions, confusions and clouded discussions to stand, the chronological interpretation allows a more authentic portrait of the thinker to emerge, with the flaws in his arguments as much part of his work as the strengths.

9.4 Religion

In the case of the concepts of religion, politics, equality and liberty, our argument against the essentialist interpretation is not that it fails to acknowledge how inconsistent Tawney is in his analysis of them, but that it fails to take account of the extent to which Tawney changed his mind over them. On the concept of religion, the chronological approach shows how the significance of the role of religion in Tawney's political thought diminished over time. This is not to deny that religion continued to have *some* place in Tawney's political theory, but more as an ideology than as a divine doctrine of truth. The seeds of this transition are sown in the *Commonplace Book* itself, which reveals that as an undergraduate, religion was a source of derision to Tawney, and it was only as he examined society's failings that he began to realize the power of its precepts. This suggests that, for Tawney, a religion's principles are to be judged at least partly on their capacity to inform practice: indeed, his eclectic approach to Christian ethical guidance blended both intuitive and consequentialist argumentation. This renders unconvincing assertions that the *Commonplace Book* contains the fundamental Christian core of Tawney's unchanging political thought, not only because there is considerable evidence to indicate that his political thought changed, but also because the Diaries do not document a settled faith, but a set of beliefs that were themselves subject to alterations.

The need to exercise caution about the essentialist assertion of the religious core to his work is demonstrated by Tawney's *Religion and the Rise of Capitalism*. In the passages where he analyses the attempt to reinvigorate Christianity as a social doctrine after its retreat to the sphere of private conduct, Tawney argues that the attempt failed because its propositions, whilst being accurate reflections of scripture, were out of kilter with a transformed society. The prescription Tawney offers, therefore, is for Christianity to adapt to social conditions; it has, like any other belief system, to be flexible to maintain relevance, rather than be a distillation of outdated pre-established dogma. This practical approach portrays Christianity as more akin to an ideology than to divine revelation, and is remote from the religious exclusivity of the Diaries that asserted the conceptual dependence of equality and duties on the existence of God. The essentialist interpretation is a one-dimensional approach that fails to acknowledge the extent to which Tawney's expressions of his religious beliefs were conditioned by his experiences.

Moreover, many of the most important of Tawney's political concepts owed less and less to his religious beliefs as his work
unfolded. For instance, his concept of Function, whilst owing an
historical debt to Christianity, was defined by Tawney in *The
Acquisitive Society* in an open-ended way, providing considerable
scope for a secular application. More specifically, the notion of
Functional property, that owners were bound by strict limitations
in the usage of their property, differed from the medieval doctrine
in that it was assertive of the entitlements of non-owners, unlike the
medieval doctrine, which Tawney emphasized was based on charity. Similarly in his discussion of the doctrine of usury, as outlined
in *Religion and the Rise of Capitalism*, Tawney stresses that it was not
purely an expression of theological dogma, but possessed an
important practical dimension relating to efficiency. There was a
rational case to be advanced to avoid exploitation, and Tawney's
position on usury was as much a reflection of his socialist sensibility as it was a product of his Christianity.

Finally, Tawney's most religious essay of his later years, *A Note
on Christianity and the Social Order*, whilst demonstrating that his
faith remained intact, was designed to persuade an already Christian audience of the virtues of radical reform, rather than to convert
the general population to Christianity and thereby to socialism.
Christianity added weight to the secular socialist message: it was
no longer for Tawney itself the sole basis of his politics.

9. 5 Politics

The gradual decline in the importance of religion in Tawney's political thought is paralleled by the gradual rise in the importance of
secular politics. Essentialist interpreters are united in accepting that
Tawney's war-time experience gave his thought a deeper institutional dynamic, with the acceptance of a greater role for the state in
stimulating and consolidating change. But what they do not
emphasize sufficiently is Tawney's changing conception of politics,

and how this impacts on the religious basis of his theory, and the orientation of his political thought in general. The *Commonplace Book* displays a profound pessimism in relation to the possibilities of politics to create an ethical order. In the Diaries, Tawney stressed that politics was immersed in the impure material realm, engaging in the pursuit of private and sectional interests which prevented it from contributing to the creation of a new moral ideal. The corrupt nature of the political state was symptomatic of the general moral malaise, rather than a cure for it. Tawney's striking analogy that the scope for modern politics to create an ethical community is akin to the capacity of a surgical procedure to eradicate air pollution, suggests that it is a categorical error to suggest that political activity can stimulate moral renewal. The early Tawney believed that certain fundamental matters should be placed beyond politics, including party politics. This depoliticization of aspects of society reflected his early view that morality is the preserve of Western European Christianity, and that conceptions of right and wrong have to express transcendental religious principles, rather than base political beliefs. The murky world of politics, concerned with interests, balancing sectional demands, and pursuing material values, cannot supply the ethical ideals to revolutionize human existence; this can only be achieved by actualizing the Christian moral framework that all decent people share. Given this dismissal of the efficacy of political institutions, and the emphasis on the need to re-engage with Christian ethics, understandably the early Tawney accords a role of particular prominence to the Church, suggesting that as the material embodiment of sanctified values, it alone can attain the necessary externality to remoralize social relations.

This deeply religious position is not confined to Tawney's Diaries: even after he has accepted that the state can play a role in pushing through vital reforms, in *The Acquisitive Society*, following a narrative that is largely secular, he gives utterance to his pre-war private thoughts by suggesting that a devotion to common ends is necessarily a religious principle and that the Church is the proper institution to propagate it. In addition, Tawney emphasizes the divisions between the faithful and pagans, stressing that the Church should not dilute its values to make a broader appeal, but stick rigidly to its elevated beliefs and seek to convert the pagans.

This mixture of religious and secular argumentation gives the impression of a thinker in flux, employing broadly political language (albeit preferring the term Functionalist to socialist), but still adhering to a fervent religiosity that makes it difficult to calculate where the balance rests.

However, Tawney's subsequent works display an increasing sympathy with politics and political institutions. From the aloofness of the mid-war essays where Tawney said the state could play its part in ethical renewal if it chose to, Tawney fully embraces the Labour Party as absolutely necessary to the creation of a new ethical order, showing a marked contrast with his pre-war condemnation of the Party's timidity and, more significantly, demonstrating that the formerly polluted political realm is now indispensable to the Good Society. The Church is now no longer the sufficient author of moral rejuvenation, or even the main institution in that endeavour. Whilst formerly Tawney had bolted concepts such as equality and liberty on to religion, by 1925 he was clear that the battle over these ideas was joined on the political terrain. For example, he emphasized in his 1934 essay, *The Choice Before the Labour Party*, that principles to guide politics were not transcendental, but based on a 'view of a life proper to human beings'. This confirms the distance travelled from the *Commonplace Book*, where concepts of right and wrong were founded on transcendental, spiritual doctrines. Tawney has shifted from a position that limited the scope of political ideologies and their agents to make meaningful moral appeals, to one where agents, specifically socialists, are essential to identifying and realizing the elevated ends that define an ethical community, despite its lack of transcendentalism and its immersion in the secular realm. To underline this transformation, Tawney transposes the values that characterized his conception of the militant Church and its uncompromising advocacy of Christianity and common ends outlined in *The Acquisitive Society*, to the Labour Party and socialism. Members of the Party must display the same resolution in adhering to their political principles as Christians display in adhering to their religious principles, regardless of short-term electoral advantage. It is secular, as opposed to religious, militancy that is now Tawney's main driver. Tawney's changing attitude to the political realm in general, and to the Labour Party in particular, represents a major shift in his thought, diluting the religious stance expressed in the Diaries. This shift cannot be explained by the essentialist interpretation of asserting an overwhelming unity, with the pre-war thought serving as the core of Tawney's subsequent theorizing.

9.6 Equality

Wright described Tawney's commitment to the equal valuation of all human beings as the 'rock of Christian principle' from which his social and moral theory derives, and suggests that we should focus on this notion, rather than upon the secular conceptual analysis that Tawney later engages in, to understand his egalitarianism. However, our chronological approach demonstrates that Tawney shifts his ground from the Christian exclusivity in relation to equal worth that is characteristic of the Diaries, to a secular inclusivity that is characteristic of his mature theory expressed in *Equality*. The former position was based on the argument that our common inferiority in relation to the Almighty is the only sound basis for human equality, and that without the positing of an omnipotent being from whom we all derive, humans will focus on their divisions, conceived in terms of superiority and inferiority. But Tawney shifts from this narrowly-based religious conception to an assertion in the first edition of *Equality* of generalized humanism that progressives, regardless of their religious beliefs, can embrace a view of common humanity that ensures that all are treated fundamentally equally.

If Tawney had maintained the rigid concept he articulated in the Diaries, his egalitarian political project would have been stillborn because he would have been unable to make an intellectually honest appeal to non-Christians: secular arguments for egalitarianism would lack the credence and authenticity that the existence of God exemplifies. By admitting that secular humanists can credibly assert the equal worth of human beings, Tawney's pre-war exclusionary conception of human valuation has been profoundly modified. This is not to deny that Tawney in the late 1930s argues that secular proponents of equal worth are influenced by Christianity, because it was initially a religious conception. But this did not constitute a reversion to the conception outlined in the Diaries because Tawney is merely acknowledging an historical derivation, not asserting a conceptual dependence. So a secular humanist advocacy of equality is no longer seen as illegitimate, although it does owe something to religion, certainly in terms of its inspiration. Moreover, Tawney's elaborate and important discussions of different distributive principles of equality—equality of opportunity, need, consideration, and outcome—arise out of his secular conceptual analysis, and owe little to a Christian-centric understanding of equal worth.

Our chronological approach, therefore, demonstrates that Tawney's notion of equal worth is developmental, and that it is only in the context of the various editions of *Equality* that his egalitarianism is explicitly developed. To reduce his detailed and unfolding prescriptions to his pre-war articulation of equal worth contained in the *Commonplace Book* is too simplistic: the political project that Tawney bequeathed to posterity would have been impossible had he maintained the conceptual exclusivity that characterizes the Diaries. So Tawney's appeal to a generalized humanism was not only a deliberate attempt to build a broad coalition of support for his egalitarian principles, but a necessary step for the working out of those principles.

9.7 Liberty

Tawney's outline of liberty in the *Commonplace Book* is brief but well-defined, expressing some themes that remained a feature of his mature political thought, such as the notion that liberty is not an end in itself, but a means to enable individuals to develop their faculties. However, when Tawney begins to discuss two concepts intimately connected with freedom—rights and duties—it becomes apparent that a general religious austerity pervades his work, with

the accent placed on meeting social obligations rather than protect-
ing a sphere of individual freedom. As a theorist who always advocated socialism as a qualitatively distinctive society in which the
place of materialism would be minimized, a residual element of
self-denial remains in his later works. However, this should not
obscure the considerable changes that Tawney's conception of liberty underwent, especially in the 1940s and 1950s. The austere,
duty-driven conception of liberty is often regarded as characteristic
of Tawney's whole corpus of thought, but it is actually confined
mainly to the *Commonplace Book* and *The Acquisitive Society*. In the
Diaries, Tawney, employing a biblical allusion, argues that rights
and duties are reconciled under the banner of the 'freedom to
serve', that is, that humans derive satisfaction from being afforded
sufficient liberties to fulfil domestic and social duties. It is in an act
of Christian subordination to the collective that we find the purpose
of mankind. Similarly, in *The Acquisitive Society*, Tawney stresses
that all rights are conditional and derivative, capable of being
waived if they conflict with social purposes; indeed, that rights
have no independent existence outside the realm of duties. Agents
are instruments of social purpose, with entitlements intimately connected to the attainment of common ends. Here, Tawney is not
interested in creating a sphere of liberty in which the individual is
free to act independently of duties; the fundamentally frivolous
have no place in this high-minded account.

However, by the 1940s, Tawney had radically modified this position, cautioning that liberty should not be too austere, with individuals having the scope to 'have their fling when they feel like it',
whilst still performing their duties, although these obligations
seem less of a Christian imposition now, as Tawney requires individuals to meet what they 'conceive their duties to be'. A greater
democratic sensibility is entering his thought, diluting the severity
and the duty-based nature of his idea of freedom. The use of the
term 'fling' demonstrates that Tawney was now tolerant of modes
of behaviour that have not directly received their rationale from
duties. This mellowing is underlined by his increasing tendency to
use the nomenclature of rights in the 1930s and, more substantially,
by his distinction between primary and secondary liberties in the
final edition of *Equality* — a distinction that fundamentally alters the

balance between rights and duties in favour of the former. Primary liberties are not contingent, not to be set aside when circumstances demanded; rather they are fundamental categories on which the *raison d'etre* of states was founded. Rights are no longer conceived as an appendage to duties; rather they had an independent existence, with society functioning around their maintenance. This position cannot be comfortably aligned with the thrust of either the Diaries or *The Acquisitive Society*, and it is too simplistic to adopt an essentialist interpretation, which fails to recognize the developmental basis of Tawney's concept of liberty away from the Christian-centric approach that characterizes his early work.

9.8 Implications for Tawney Studies

If our central contention that Tawney's thought is characterized by considerable change, mainly expressed in a dilution of the Christian influence on his key concepts, is accepted, then it has important implications for future Tawney scholarship. It shows that the essentialist approach to Tawney is seriously flawed, creating the impression of a systematic theorist who outlined a set of political concepts which he largely adhered to throughout a long academic career. Indeed, Terrill openly states that the creation of a systematic Tawney is necessary to aid our understanding of his ideas. However, given the extent of the transformation, and the range of concepts that are changed, the essentialist approach is reductive, and fails to appreciate the significance of Tawney's intellectual trajectory. Far from aiding our understanding, the assumption of a systematic basis diminishes our comprehension, creating a partial and abstract Tawney — possibly even a fictitious Tawney. Our chronological analysis of Tawney's publications reveals such profound alterations in his views on religion, politics, equality, liberty, rights, and duties, that the attempt to minimize those changes does him an unintended disservice.

Bibliography

Annan, N. (1990) *Our Age*, London: Fontana.

Baker, J. (1996) *Arguing for Equality*, London: Verso.

Barry, N.P. (1989) *An Introduction to Modern Political Theory*, London: Macmillan.

Berlin, I (2002), *Liberty*, ed. with an introduction by Hardy, H., Cornwall: Oxford University Press.

Carter, M. (2003) *T.H. Green and the Development of Ethical Socialism*, Exeter: Imprint Academic.

Chambers, J.D. (1971) 'The Tawney tradition' *Economic History Review*, Second Series, XXIV (3): 355–369.

Cliff, B. & Tomlinson, J. (2002) 'Tawney and the third way' *Journal of Political Ideologies*, 7 (3): 315–331.

Collini, S. (1998) 'Reconsiderations: *The Acquisitive Society*' *Dissent*, Summer: 93–99.

Crewe, I. & King, A. (1995) *The Birth, Life and Death of the Social Democratic Party*, Oxford: Oxford University Press.

Dale, G. (2000) *God's Politicians: The Christian Contribution to 100 Years of Labour*, London: Harper Collins.

Dell, E. (2000) *A Strange and Eventful History: Democratic Socialism in Britain*, London: Harper Collins.

Dennis, N. & Halsey, A.H. (1988) *English Ethical Socialism*, Oxford: Clarendon Press.

Duff, A. (2004) 'The Sickness of an Information Society' *Information, Communication and Society*, 7 (3): 403–422.

Durbin, E. (1985) *The New Jerusalem: The Labour Party and the Economics of Democratic Socialism*, London: Routledge and Kegan Paul.

Foote, G. (1985) *The Labour Party's Political Thought*, London: Croomhelm.

Freeden, M. (1986) *Liberalism Divided: A Study in British Political Thought 1914–1939*, Oxford: Clarendon Press.

Greenleaf, W.H. (1983) *The British Political Tradition Volume Two: The Ideological Tradition*, London: Routledge.

Hattersley, R. (1987) *Choose Freedom: The Future for Democratic Socialism*, London: Michael Joseph.

Hayek, F (1944) *The Road to Serfdom*, Chicago: Chicago University Press.

Hinden, R. (ed.) (1964) *The Radical Tradition*, London: George Allen & Unwin.

Honderich, T. (1991) *Conservatism*, London: Penguin.

Hutchinson, F. & Burkitt, B. (1997) *The Political Economy of Social Credit and Guild Socialism*, London: Routledge.

James, R.R. (1978) *The British Revolution*, London: Hamish Hamilton.

Joseph, K. & Sumption, J. (1979) *Equality*, London: John Murray.

Kinnock, N.G. (1986) *Making Our Way: Investing in Britain's Future*, Oxford: Blackwell.

Kramnick, I. & Sheerman, B. (1993) *Harold Laski: A Life on the Left*, London: Hamish Hamilton.

Marquand, D. (1999) *The Progressive Dilemma: From Lloyd George to Blair*, London: Phoenix.

Orwell, G. (1989) *The Road to Wigan Pier*, Harmondsworth: Penguin.

Pimlott, B. (1992) *Harold Wilson*, London: Harper Collins.

Raeburn, A. (1974) *The Militant Suffragettes*, London: Michael Joseph.

Reisman, D. (1987) *State & Welfare: Tawney, Galbraith & Adam Smith*, London: Macmillan.

Ryan, A. (1980) 'A socialist saint' *New Statesman*, 54 (941): 408–410, 27/11/1980.

Sassoon, D. (1997) *One Hundred Years of Socialism*, London: Fontana.

Skinner, Q. (1969) 'Meaning and understanding in the history of ideas' *History and Theory*, 8 (1): 3–53.

Tawney, R.H. (1910-1914) *The New Leviathan*, Tawney Archive, London: London School of Economics. [Unpublished manuscript].

Tawney, R.H. (1913) 'Poverty as an industrial problem' in *History and Society: Essays by R.H. Tawney* (1978), London: Routledge and Kegan Paul.

Tawney, R.H. (1915) *Minimum Rates in the Tailoring Industry*, London: G. Bell & Sons Ltd.

Tawney, R.H. (1916) 'The attack' in *The Attack* (1953), London: Spokesman University Paperback.

Tawney, R.H. (1916) 'Some reflections of a soldier' in *The Attack* (1953), London: Spokesman University Paperback.

Tawney, R.H. (1917) 'A national college of all souls' in *The Attack* (1953), London: Spokesman University Paperback.

Tawney, R.H. (1918) 'The conditions of economic liberty' in *The Radical Tradition* (1964b), London: George Allen & Unwin.

Tawney, R.H. (1920) *The Sickness of an Acquisitive Society*, The Fabian Society, London: George Allen & Unwin.

Tawney, R.H. (1921) *The Acquisitive Society*, London: G. Bell & Sons Ltd.

Tawney, R.H. (1924) *Education: The Socialist Policy*, London: Independent Labour Party.

Tawney, R.H. (1931) *Equality*, London: George Allen & Unwin.

Tawney, R.H. (1934) 'The choice before the Labour Party' in *The Attack* (1953), London: Spokesman University Paperback.

Tawney, R.H. (1937) 'A note on Christianity and the social order' in *The Attack* (1953), London: Spokesman University Paperback.

Tawney, R.H. (1937) *Land and Labour in China*, London: George Allen & Unwin.

Tawney, R.H. (1938) *Equality*, London: George Allen & Unwin. [Second edition].

Tawney, R.H. (1940) 'Why Britain fights' in *The Attack* (1953), London: Spokesman University Paperback.

Tawney, R.H. (1943) 'Beatrice Webb, 1858–1943' in *The Radical Tradition* (1964b), London: George Allen & Unwin.

Tawney, R.H. (1944) 'We mean freedom' in *The Radical Tradition* (1964b), London: George Allen & Unwin.

Tawney, R.H. (1949) 'Social democracy in Britain' in *The Radical Tradition* (1964b), London: George Allen & Unwin.

Tawney, R.H. (1952) 'British socialism today' in *The Radical Tradition* (1964b), London: George Allen & Unwin.

Tawney, R.H. (1953) *The Attack*, introduction by Benn, T., London: Spokesman University Paperback. [Includes *The Attack* (1916); *Some Reflections of a Soldier* (1916); *A National College of All Souls* (1917); *The Choice before the Labour Party* (1934); *A Note on Christianity and the Social Order* (1937); *Why Britain Fights* (1940)].

Tawney, R.H. (1958) *Business and Politics Under James I: Lionel Cranfield as Merchant and Minister*, Cambridge: Cambridge University Press.

Tawney, R.H. (1961) *Letter to D. F. J. Parsons*, Tawney/Vyvyan 16, LSE Archive.

Tawney, R. H. (1961) *Letter to Miss I Gandy*, Tawney/Vyvyan Archive 15, LSE Archive.

Tawney, R. H. (1961) *Letter to Father Larkin*, Tawney/Vyvyan 16, LSE Archive.

Tawney, R.H. (1964a) *Equality*, introduction by Titmuss, R., London: George Allen & Unwin. [Reprint of third edition, first published in 1952].

Tawney, R.H. (1964b) *The Radical Tradition*, ed. Hinden, R., with an Appreciation by Gaitskill, H., London: George Allen & Unwin. [Includes *The Conditions of Economic Liberty* (1918); *Beatrice Webb, 1858–1943* (1943); *We Mean Freedom* (1944); *Social Democracy in Britain* (1949); *British Socialism Today* (1952)].

Tawney, R.H. (1967) *The Agrarian Problem in the Sixteenth Century*, New York: Harper Torchbooks.

Tawney, R.H. (1968) *The British Labour Movement*, New York: Greenwood Press. [First published in 1925].

Tawney, R.H. (1972) *R.H. Tawney's Commonplace Book*, ed. with an introduction by Winter, J.M. & Joslin, D.M., Cambridge: Cambridge University Press. [Also known as the 'Diaries' — written in 1912–1914, but unpublished during Tawney's lifetime].

Tawney, R.H. (1978) *History and Society: Essays by R.H. Tawney*, ed. with an introduction by Winter, J.M., London: Routledge and Kegan Paul. [Includes *Poverty as an Industrial Problem* (1913); *The Study of Economic History* (1933)].

Tawney, R.H. (1979) *The American Labour Movement and other Essays*, ed. Winter, J.M., London: Harvester.

Tawney, R.H. (1988) *Secondary Education for All: A Policy for Labour*, ed. and introduced by Brooks, J.R., London: Hambledon Press. [First published as a Labour Party policy document in 1922].

Tawney, R.H. (1990) *Religion and the Rise of Capitalism*, Harmondsworth: Penguin. [First published 1926].

Terrill, R. (1973) *R.H. Tawney and his Times: Socialism as Fellowship*, Cambridge, MA: Harvard University Press.

Titmuss, R., Williams, J.R. & Fisher, F.J. (1960) *R.H. Tawney: A Portrait by Several Hands*, privately published.

Trevor-Roper, H.R. (1959) *The Gentry 1540–1640*, London: Cambridge University Press.

Webb, B. (1978) *Modern England*, London: George Allen & Unwin.

Williams, R. (1961) *Culture and Society 1780–1950*, Edinburgh: Penguin.

Williams, S. (1981) *Politics is for People*, Cambridge: Cambridge University Press.

Winter, J.M. (ed.) (1972) *R.H. Tawney's Commonplace Book*, Cambridge: Cambridge University Press.

Winter, J.M. (1974) *Socialism and the Challenge of War: Ideas and Politics in Britain 1912–1918*, London: Routledge and Kegan Paul.

Wootton, B. (1952) 'Return to Equality?' *Political Quarterly*, 23 (1–4): 261–268.

Wright, A. (1987) *R.H. Tawney*, Manchester: Manchester University Press.

Index

Note that this index does not include entries for 'Tawney', because the author's name appears on virtually every page.